# JUDAS MACCABEUS

# JUDAS MACCABEUS

E. H. Fortier

CHELSEA HOUSE PUBLISHERS
NEW YORK
PHILADELPHIA

**Chelsea House Publishers**
EDITOR-IN-CHIEF: Nancy Toff
EXECUTIVE EDITOR: Remmel T. Nunn
MANAGING EDITOR: Karyn Gullen Browne
COPY CHIEF: Juliann Barbato
PICTURE EDITOR: Adrian G. Allen
ART DIRECTOR: Giannella Garrett
MANUFACTURING MANAGER: Gerald Levine

**World Leaders—Past & Present**
SENIOR EDITOR: John W. Selfridge

**Staff for JUDAS MACCABEUS:**
ASSOCIATE EDITOR: Jeff Klein
DEPUTY COPY CHIEF: Ellen Scordato
EDITORIAL ASSISTANTS: Sean Ginty, Wendy Van Wyck
PICTURE RESEARCHERS: Alan Gottlieb, Lynn Goldberg
SENIOR DESIGNER: Ghila Krajzman
PRODUCTION COORDINATOR: Joseph Romano
COVER ILLUSTRATION: Peter McCaffrey

3  5  7  9  8  6  4  2

Library of Congress Cataloging in Publication Data

Fortier, E. H.
Judas Maccabeus.

p.   cm.—(World leaders past & present)
Bibliography: p.
Includes index.
   Summary: Presents a biography of the Jewish leader who led the revolt
against the Seleucid Empire, taking Jerusalem in 164 B.C. and
rededicating the Temple.
ISBN 0-87754-539-1
      0-7910-0653-0 (pbk.)

1. Judas, Maccabeus, d. 161 B.C.—Juvenile literature.
2. Jews—History—168 B.C.—A.D. 135—Juvenile literature.
3. Jews—Kings and rulers—Biography—Juvenile literature.
4. Jews—Palestine—Biography—Juvenile literature.
5. Palestine—Biography—Juvenile literature. [1. Judas,
Maccabeus, d. 161 B.C. 2. Jews—History—168 B.C.—A.D. 135
3. Kings, queens, rulers, etc.] I. Title. II. Series.
DS121.8.J8F67     1988
933'.04'0924—dc19                              88-6098
[B]                                            CIP
[92]                                           AC

# Contents

JOHN ADAMS
JOHN QUINCY ADAMS
KONRAD ADENAUER
ALEXANDER THE GREAT
SALVADOR ALLENDE
MARC ANTONY
CORAZON AQUINO
YASIR ARAFAT
KING ARTHUR
HAFEZ AL-ASSAD
KEMAL ATATÜRK
ATTILA
CLEMENT ATTLEE
AUGUSTUS CAESAR
MENACHEM BEGIN
DAVID BEN-GURION
OTTO VON BISMARCK
LÉON BLUM
SIMON BOLÍVAR
CESARE BORGIA
WILLY BRANDT
LEONID BREZHNEV
JULIUS CAESAR
JOHN CALVIN
JIMMY CARTER
FIDEL CASTRO
CATHERINE THE GREAT
CHARLEMAGNE
CHIANG KAI-SHEK
WINSTON CHURCHILL
GEORGES CLEMENCEAU
CLEOPATRA
CONSTANTINE THE GREAT
HERNÁN CORTÉS
OLIVER CROMWELL
GEORGES-JACQUES
   DANTON
JEFFERSON DAVIS
MOSHE DAYAN
CHARLES DE GAULLE
EAMON DE VALERA
EUGENE DEBS
DENG XIAOPING
BENJAMIN DISRAELI
ALEXANDER DUBČEK
FRANÇOIS & JEAN-CLAUDE
   DUVALIER
DWIGHT EISENHOWER
ELEANOR OF AQUITAINE
ELIZABETH I
FAISAL
FERDINAND & ISABELLA
FRANCISCO FRANCO
BENJAMIN FRANKLIN

FREDERICK THE GREAT
INDIRA GANDHI
MOHANDAS GANDHI
GIUSEPPE GARIBALDI
AMIN & BASHIR GEMAYEL
GENGHIS KHAN
WILLIAM GLADSTONE
MIKHAIL GORBACHEV
ULYSSES S. GRANT
ERNESTO "CHE" GUEVARA
TENZIN GYATSO
ALEXANDER HAMILTON
DAG HAMMARSKJÖLD
HENRY VIII
HENRY OF NAVARRE
PAUL VON HINDENBURG
HIROHITO
ADOLF HITLER
HO CHI MINH
KING HUSSEIN
IVAN THE TERRIBLE
ANDREW JACKSON
JAMES I
WOJCIECH JARUZELSKI
THOMAS JEFFERSON
JOAN OF ARC
POPE JOHN XXIII
POPE JOHN PAUL II
LYNDON JOHNSON
BENITO JUÁREZ
JOHN KENNEDY
ROBERT KENNEDY
JOMO KENYATTA
AYATOLLAH KHOMEINI
NIKITA KHRUSHCHEV
KIM IL SUNG
MARTIN LUTHER KING, JR.
HENRY KISSINGER
KUBLAI KHAN
LAFAYETTE
ROBERT E. LEE
VLADIMIR LENIN
ABRAHAM LINCOLN
DAVID LLOYD GEORGE
LOUIS XIV
MARTIN LUTHER
JUDAS MACCABEUS
JAMES MADISON
NELSON & WINNIE
   MANDELA
MAO ZEDONG
FERDINAND MARCOS
GEORGE MARSHALL

MARY, QUEEN OF SCOTS
TOMÁŠ MASARYK
GOLDA MEIR
KLEMENS VON METTERNICH
JAMES MONROE
HOSNI MUBARAK
ROBERT MUGABE
BENITO MUSSOLINI
NAPOLÉON BONAPARTE
GAMAL ABDEL NASSER
JAWAHARLAL NEHRU
NERO
NICHOLAS II
RICHARD NIXON
KWAME NKRUMAH
DANIEL ORTEGA
MOHAMMED REZA PAHLAVI
THOMAS PAINE
CHARLES STEWART
   PARNELL
PERICLES
JUAN PERÓN
PETER THE GREAT
POL POT
MUAMMAR EL-QADDAFI
RONALD REAGAN
CARDINAL RICHELIEU
MAXIMILIEN ROBESPIERRE
ELEANOR ROOSEVELT
FRANKLIN ROOSEVELT
THEODORE ROOSEVELT
ANWAR SADAT
HAILE SELASSIE
PRINCE SIHANOUK
JAN SMUTS
JOSEPH STALIN
SUKARNO
SUN YAT-SEN
TAMERLANE
MOTHER TERESA
MARGARET THATCHER
JOSIP BROZ TITO
TOUSSAINT L'OUVERTURE
LEON TROTSKY
PIERRE TRUDEAU
HARRY TRUMAN
QUEEN VICTORIA
LECH WALESA
GEORGE WASHINGTON
CHAIM WEIZMANN
WOODROW WILSON
XERXES
EMILIANO ZAPATA
ZHOU ENLAI

CHELSEA HOUSE PUBLISHERS

# ON LEADERSHIP

*Arthur M. Schlesinger, jr.*

LEADERSHIP, it may be said, is really what makes the world go round. Love no doubt smooths the passage; but love is a private transaction between consenting adults. Leadership is a public transaction with history. The idea of leadership affirms the capacity of individuals to move, inspire, and mobilize masses of people so that they act together in pursuit of an end. Sometimes leadership serves good purposes, sometimes bad; but whether the end is benign or evil, great leaders are those men and women who leave their personal stamp on history.

Now, the very concept of leadership implies the proposition that individuals can make a difference. This proposition has never been universally accepted. From classical times to the present day, eminent thinkers have regarded individuals as no more than the agents and pawns of larger forces, whether the gods and goddesses of the ancient world or, in the modern era, race, class, nation, the dialectic, the will of the people, the spirit of the times, history itself. Against such forces, the individual dwindles into insignificance.

So contends the thesis of historical determinism. Tolstoy's great novel *War and Peace* offers a famous statement of the case. Why, Tolstoy asked, did millions of men in the Napoleonic Wars, denying their human feelings and their common sense, move back and forth across Europe slaughtering their fellows? "The war," Tolstoy answered, "was bound to happen simply because it was bound to happen." All prior history predetermined it. As for leaders, they, Tolstoy said, "are but the labels that serve to give a name to an end and, like labels, they have the least possible connection with the event." The greater the leader, "the more conspicuous the inevitability and the predestination of every act he commits." The leader, said Tolstoy, is "the slave of history."

Determinism takes many forms. Marxism is the determinism of class. Nazism the determinism of race. But the idea of men and women as the slaves of history runs athwart the deepest human instincts. Rigid determinism abolishes the idea of human freedom—

the assumption of free choice that underlies every move we make, every word we speak, every thought we think. It abolishes the idea of human responsibility, since it is manifestly unfair to reward or punish people for actions that are by definition beyond their control. No one can live consistently by any deterministic creed. The Marxist states prove this themselves by their extreme susceptibility to the cult of leadership.

More than that, history refutes the idea that individuals make no difference. In December 1931 a British politician crossing Park Avenue in New York City between 76th and 77th Streets around 10:30 P.M. looked in the wrong direction and was knocked down by an automobile—a moment, he later recalled, of a man aghast, a world aglare: "I do not understand why I was not broken like an eggshell or squashed like a gooseberry." Fourteen months later an American politician, sitting in an open car in Miami, Florida, was fired on by an assassin; the man beside him was hit. Those who believe that individuals make no difference to history might well ponder whether the next two decades would have been the same had Mario Constasino's car killed Winston Churchill in 1931 and Giuseppe Zangara's bullet killed Franklin Roosevelt in 1933. Suppose, in addition, that Adolf Hitler had been killed in the street fighting during the Munich *Putsch* of 1923 and that Lenin had died of typhus during World War I. What would the 20th century be like now?

For better or for worse, individuals do make a difference. "The notion that a people can run itself and its affairs anonymously," wrote the philosopher William James, "is now well known to be the silliest of absurdities. Mankind does nothing save through initiatives on the part of inventors, great or small, and imitation by the rest of us—these are the sole factors in human progress. Individuals of genius show the way, and set the patterns, which common people then adopt and follow."

Leadership, James suggests, means leadership in thought as well as in action. In the long run, leaders in thought may well make the greater difference to the world. But, as Woodrow Wilson once said, "Those only are leaders of men, in the general eye, who lead in action. . . . It is at their hands that new thought gets its translation into the crude language of deeds." Leaders in thought often invent in solitude and obscurity, leaving to later generations the tasks of imitation. Leaders in action—the leaders portrayed in this series—have to be effective in their own time.

And they cannot be effective by themselves. They must act in response to the rhythms of their age. Their genius must be adapted, in a phrase of William James's, "to the receptivities of the moment." Leaders are useless without followers. "There goes the mob," said the French politician hearing a clamor in the streets. "I am their leader. I must follow them." Great leaders turn the inchoate emotions of the mob to purposes of their own. They seize on the opportunities of their time, the hopes, fears, frustrations, crises, potentialities. They succeed when events have prepared the way for them, when the community is awaiting to be aroused, when they can provide the clarifying and organizing ideas. Leadership ignites the circuit between the individual and the mass and thereby alters history.

It may alter history for better or for worse. Leaders have been responsible for the most extravagant follies and most monstrous crimes that have beset suffering humanity. They have also been vital in such gains as humanity has made in individual freedom, religious and racial tolerance, social justice, and respect for human rights.

There is no sure way to tell in advance who is going to lead for good and who for evil. But a glance at the gallery of men and women in *World Leaders—Past and Present* suggests some useful tests.

One test is this: Do leaders lead by force or by persuasion? By command or by consent? Through most of history leadership was exercised by the divine right of authority. The duty of followers was to defer and to obey. "Theirs not to reason why / Theirs but to do and die." On occasion, as with the so-called enlightened despots of the 18th century in Europe, absolutist leadership was animated by humane purposes. More often, absolutism nourished the passion for domination, land, gold, and conquest and resulted in tyranny.

The great revolution of modern times has been the revolution of equality. The idea that all people should be equal in their legal condition has undermined the old structure of authority, hierarchy, and deference. The revolution of equality has had two contrary effects on the nature of leadership. For equality, as Alexis de Tocqueville pointed out in his great study *Democracy in America*, might mean equality in servitude as well as equality in freedom.

"I know of only two methods of establishing equality in the political world," Tocqueville wrote. "Rights must be given to every citizen, or none at all to anyone . . . save one, who is the master of all." There was no middle ground "between the sovereignty of all and the absolute power of one man." In his astonishing prediction of 20th-century totalitarian dictatorship, Tocqueville explained how the revolution of equality could lead to the *"Führerprinzip"* and more terrible absolutism than the world had ever known.

But when rights are given to every citizen and the sovereignty of all is established, the problem of leadership takes a new form, becomes more exacting than ever before. It is easy to issue commands and enforce them by the rope and the stake, the concentration camp and the *gulag.* It is much harder to use argument and achievement to overcome opposition and win consent. The Founding Fathers of the United States understood the difficulty. They believed that history had given them the opportunity to decide, as Alexander Hamilton wrote in the first Federalist Paper, whether men are indeed capable of basing government on "reflection and choice, or whether they are forever destined to depend . . . on accident and force."

Government by reflection and choice called for a new style of leadership and a new quality of followership. It required leaders to be responsive to popular concerns, and it required followers to be active and informed participants in the process. Democracy does not eliminate emotion from politics; sometimes it fosters demagoguery; but it is confident that, as the greatest of democratic leaders put it, you cannot fool all of the people all of the time. It measures leadership by results and retires those who overreach or falter or fail.

It is true that in the long run despots are measured by results too. But they can postpone the day of judgment, sometimes indefinitely, and in the meantime they can do infinite harm. It is also true that democracy is no guarantee of virtue and intelligence in government, for the voice of the people is not necessarily the voice of God. But democracy, by assuring the right of opposition, offers built-in resistance to the evils inherent in absolutism. As the theologian Reinhold Niebuhr summed it up, "Man's capacity for justice makes democracy possible, but man's inclination to injustice makes democracy necessary."

A second test for leadership is the end for which power is sought. When leaders have as their goal the supremacy of a master race or the promotion of totalitarian revolution or the acquisition and exploitation of colonies or the protection of greed and privilege or the preservation of personal power, it is likely that their leadership will do little to advance the cause of humanity. When their goal is the abolition of slavery, the liberation of women, the enlargement of opportunity for the poor and powerless, the extension of equal rights to racial minorities, the defense of the freedoms of expression and opposition, it is likely that their leadership will increase the sum of human liberty and welfare.

Leaders have done great harm to the world. They have also conferred great benefits. You will find both sorts in this series. Even "good" leaders must be regarded with a certain wariness. Leaders are not demigods; they put on their trousers one leg after another just like ordinary mortals. No leader is infallible, and every leader needs to be reminded of this at regular intervals. Irreverence irritates leaders but is their salvation. Unquestioning submission corrupts leaders and demeans followers. Making a cult of a leader is always a mistake. Fortunately hero worship generates its own antidote. "Every hero," said Emerson, "becomes a bore at last."

The signal benefit the great leaders confer is to embolden the rest of us to live according to our own best selves, to be active, insistent, and resolute in affirming our own sense of things. For great leaders attest to the reality of human freedom against the supposed inevitabilities of history. And they attest to the wisdom and power that may lie within the most unlikely of us, which is why Abraham Lincoln remains the supreme example of great leadership. A great leader, said Emerson, exhibits new possibilities to all humanity. "We feed on genius. . . . Great men exist that there may be greater men."

Great leaders, in short, justify themselves by emancipating and empowering their followers. So humanity struggles to master its destiny, remembering with Alexis de Tocqueville: "It is true that around every man a fatal circle is traced beyond which he cannot pass; but within the wide verge of that circle he is powerful and free; as it is with man, so with communities."

# 1

# The Battle of Emmaus

Judas Maccabeus, the leader of an army of Judean rebels, stood on a bluff overlooking the plain by the town of Emmaus and waited for dawn. Below him, the Seleucid imperial army, some 20,000 strong, lay in wait. Watch fires dotted the dark valley floor around the Seleucid camp, where Nicanor, the Seleucid general, was preparing to move against the Judean rebels. He was under orders to kill Judah Maccabee, as Judas Maccabeus was called in Hebrew and Aramaic, the languages of the Judeans. The Seleucid Empire was certain that if Judah Maccabee were dead, the revolt for freedom in Judea would die too.

It was June 165 B.C. Judea, part of what is today Israel, had for 33 years been ruled by the Seleucid Empire, whose territories stretched from what is now Turkey in the north and west, to the Sinai desert in the south, to present-day Iran in the east. During the first three decades of Seleucid rule of Judea, the native inhabitants, the Jews, were allowed to practice their customs and religion. But now the Seleucid king, Antiochus IV Epiphanes, resolved to force Hellenism (Greek customs and religion) on the Jews, in spite of the Jews' fierce devotion to their religion.

*For they [the Seleucid troops] trust in their weapons and boldness; but our confidence is in the Almighty God, who at a beck can cast down both them that come against us, and also all the world.*
—JUDAH MACCABEE
from 2 Maccabees

**Judah Maccabee as depicted in a 16th-century manuscript. The revolt he led against the Seleucid Empire — recorded in 1 and 2 Maccabees, two books that form part of the Christian Bible — eventually won religious and political independence for the Jewish province of Judea.**

Judah Maccabee, while looking down on the watch fires of the Seleucid army, may have thought back to the time three years earlier, in 168 B.C., when the Seleucid king cruelly put down an uprising in Jerusalem. Antiochus IV marched into Jerusalem and attacked devout Jews who refused to observe Hellenism. These Jews did not carry weapons, believing that to do so would profane the law of God. They were slaughtered by the thousands, their homes burned, their wives and children sold into slavery. Those who could fled Jerusalem for the countryside.

Then Antiochus IV looted the Temple, the Jews' most sacred place of worship. He stripped it to the bare walls, carrying away all its holy treasures. In the holiest sanctuary of the Temple he placed a statue of Zeus, king of the Greek gods. He ordered the Jews to sacrifice pigs to Zeus on the Temple altar and to eat pork in deliberate violation of Jewish law, which forbade the eating of pork or even the touching of pigs. Drunken Seleucid soldiers reveled with prostitutes in the Temple, and beside it the Seleucids built a huge fortress, called the Acra, which was filled with soldiers to enforce the king's orders.

**The probable site of the Battle of Emmaus as it appears today. In 165 B.C. the outnumbered Maccabean forces, rushing down from the bluffs, attacked and routed the Seleucid army while it was still encamped on the plain below.**

In 167 B.C., Antiochus IV decreed that all Jews must stop observing the Torah, Jewish religious law as set down in the five books of Moses, which, hundreds of years later, would become the first five books of the Old Testament. Under Antiochus IV's decree, Jews were forbidden to read the Torah and it was burned wherever Seleucid officials found copies. Jews who resisted and continued to practice their religion or even read the Torah were tortured to death, along with their families.

Imperial agents carried the decree throughout Judea, including the small village of Modin, 17 miles northwest of Jerusalem. Modin was the home of an old priest, Mattathias, and his five sons. When the imperial agents arrived in the village, Mattathias led a small uprising that soon grew into a full-scale Jewish revolt against Seleucid tyranny. He died a few months after the start of the rebellion. Judah, the third of his five sons, stepped forward to lead the revolt.

Now, with morning a faint glow on the horizon, Judah faced the most important battle of the revolt. The price of losing, he knew, was death for himself and slavery for his people. But more important, it could mean the end of the Jewish religion.

Judah and his ragged army of 3,000 had spent the previous day praying and fasting in their camp at Mizpah. Judah realized that Nicanor, the Seleucid general, knew the location of his camp. So in the middle of the night, Judah led his rebel army quietly away from Mizpah, leaving their tents up and their campfires burning. He hoped Nicanor would believe that the Jewish troops were still at Mizpah. Judah's army crept silently through the brush of the rugged foothills for 10 miles, until they reached a bluff overlooking Nicanor's encamped army.

The Seleucid camp sprawled before Judah and his men, spread on the plain beside the town of Emmaus. Several hundred of the 20,000 soldiers it held were cavalrymen. Many of the 20,000 were imperial troops, the best soldiers of the empire; others were Idumaeans and Philistines, local garrison forces

P. Bodart. fr

ANTIOCHUS
EPIPHA

In 167 B.C. Antiochus IV Epiphanes, king of the Seleucid Empire, forced the Jews to worship the Greek gods and abolished the Jewish religion. Despite severe enforcement measures, the Jews of Judea resisted; within a year they were in open revolt against the empire.

that had joined the imperial army for the expedition. The camp also held cavalry horses, packhorses, camp followers, and slave merchants, who were so sure of a Seleucid victory that they had already posted prices for the Jews they anticipated would be captured in battle. After all, Judah's army was outnumbered by almost seven to one. Nonetheless, the Seleucids had taken the precaution of posting mounted sentries to patrol the perimeter of the camp. The camp was further protected by a deep, encircling trench into which the Seleucids had driven sharply pointed stakes.

Judah planned to ambush Nicanor's army as it moved to attack his abandoned camp at Mizpah. In the rugged hills and steep ravines the small Jewish army would at least have a chance against the Seleucids. But as the Judean scouts surveyed the Seleucid camp and the surrounding countryside, they saw to their astonishment that the enemy had made a critical tactical error.

Nicanor had ordered Gorgias, his second in command, to attack the Mizpah camp during the night. Judah's scouts watched as Gorgias took as many as 5,000 men and 1,000 cavalry and spent the night stumbling along the narrow, rocky trails. The overconfident Seleucid army was now divided in the plain below the Jewish forces. Still, Nicanor had an effective advantage of at least five soldiers for each Jewish soldier.

Judah's scouts told him of Nicanor's mistake when he left the bluff and returned to the Judean camp. The time was right for Judah's own attack, and when his men were fed and armed, they moved out.

Shortly thereafter, Gorgias arrived at Mizpah to find the Judean camp abandoned. He assumed that the Jews had heard his soldiers marching through the woods and fled into the surrounding mountains. Gorgias wanted the glory of crushing the Jewish army himself, so, instead of returning to Emmaus, he ordered his men to spread out and comb the surrounding countryside to hunt down the Jewish soldiers he thought were trying to escape.

Antiochus IV ordered the sacking of Jerusalem in both
168 and 167 B.C., resulting in the massacre of thousands
of civilians and the desecration of the Temple, which was
turned into a shrine to the Greek god Zeus. The figures
in this 14th-century illustration wear Renaissance dress.

Meanwhile, in the growing light of dawn at Emmaus, the alarmed Seleucid guards woke the troops, only to find Judah's soldiers prepared for battle on the high ground above the camp. The surprised Seleucid troops rushed to strap on their armor and grab their swords and spears. They were equipped with the latest military gear: bronze breastplates, wooden shields overlaid with hammered brass, leg guards, and large bronze helmets that protected their cheeks and noses. They carried iron swords and 18-foot-long iron-tipped spears.

Against these Judah stood with his poor and ragged bunch, armed with pruning hooks, slings, bows and arrows, and any other homemade weapons they could find. A few Jews wore pieces of Seleucid armor and weaponry they had captured in previous battles.

Nicanor's army marched from its camp in disciplined rows. Judah shouted encouragement to his troops, saying, "Have no fear of their numbers and do not be dismayed at their onslaught. . . . He [God] will smash this army before us today, so that all Gentiles will know that there is a Redeemer and Savior of Israel." While half the Seleucid troops were still inside their camp, the Judean army poured down the hillside, shouting and blowing *shofars*, trumpets made from rams' horns.

The Judean assault, spurred by religious fervor, was so strong that it shattered the disciplined Seleucid ranks. Nicanor's soldiers were pushed back, many of them tumbling into the moat bristling with sharpened stakes that had been meant to defend them. Others threw down their weapons and ran. The Maccabeans poured into the Seleucid camp, driving everyone before them. The Seleucids, who had been so certain of an easy victory, now panicked in the face of the Judean assault. Screams, war cries, and dust filled the morning; camp tents, set afire by the Maccabees, sent choking plumes of smoke through the camp. The terrified Seleucids abandoned their camp and fled.

But Judah knew that he could not stop now. The main Seleucid army, still many times larger than

The *shofar*, or ram's horn, was used by Jews both in religious ceremonies and military campaigns. Judah Maccabee used shofars to sound the signal for ambushes in the early battles of the revolt against the Seleucid Empire.

his own, could easily regroup and return, and Gorgias's men were somewhere in the foothills. So Judah allowed his men to chase the disintegrating Seleucid army to Gezara, six miles away. More than 3,000 Seleucid soldiers died in Judah's attack on Emmaus and the chase to Gezara. Quickly reassembling his troops, Judah marched back to Emmaus.

Gorgias's men were tired; they had searched the rough hills all night, and the hot weather did not help — the wind that blows off the Arabian desert in June is often as hot as 120 degrees. Late in the day, nearing Emmaus, they saw rising smoke from the still-burning camp, occupied not by the imperial army, but by victorious Jewish troops. This sight,

This platter, dating from the 5th century B.C., depicts Greek soldiers killing a woman. Antiochus IV sent soldiers throughout Judea with orders to torture and kill all who refused to abandon Judaism and adopt the worship of Zeus. The decrees and the ferocity of their enforcement touched off the Maccabean revolt.

after a night and part of a day spent stumbling through the rough countryside, must have filled Gorgias's troops with dismay.

Gorgias was convinced that the Jewish troops were looting what was left of the Seleucid camp, taking anything of value, as was the standard practice of armies at that time. He believed that the Jewish troops would be too busy looting to see his army approach. At his command, his troops rushed down on the camp at Emmaus.

But Judah had forbidden his men to loot the camp. Instead, he held them in battle position, ready for the attack from Gorgias. As Gorgias's men ran toward the camp, they saw the Maccabean soldiers behind the camp's barriers prepared and, after their defeat of Nicanor, eager for battle. Hot, tired, hungry, discouraged, and facing an enemy in firm control of a defensive position, Gorgias and his troops turned and ran without a fight.

The Maccabees had won a major victory in the war to free Judea. They celebrated amid the ruins of the Seleucid camp. They found treasure chests full of gold and silver coins that had belonged to the hated slave merchants, and bolts of cloth dyed with such expensive colors that the cloth was nearly as valuable as gold. More important, they found Seleucid armor and weapons, almost enough to supply their entire army. They returned to their own camp praising God and singing hymns of thanksgiving.

Joy and excitement spread throughout Judea at the news of the victory over the Seleucid army. Jews everywhere in the province sang the praises of Judah Maccabee.

> He was like a lion in his deeds
> And like the king of the beasts
> roaring over his prey.

The defeated Seleucids locked themselves behind the walls of the Acra in Jerusalem while Judah, the Lion of Judea, commanded the countryside. Before the Battle of Emmaus, few people believed that Judea could be free, but now this hope spread. New soldiers flocked to join Judah's army, and it grew to 10,000 men. But Antiochus IV, king of the Seleucids, would not admit defeat that easily. Judah knew that much more blood would have to be spilled before his people could be free.

# 2
# Hellenism and the Seleucids

The Seleucid Empire was one of the successors to the huge but short-lived empire of Alexander the Great, a young Macedonian Greek who conquered all the lands from Greece and the Balkans, south through Syria and Palestine (the region that included Judea) to Egypt, and east through Persia into India. The extent of Alexander's conquests, made between 336 and 323 B.C., was unprecedented in world history. Even compared to later domains it remains one of the largest empires ever amassed.

Prior to Alexander, most conquerors were usually unconcerned with the culture and religion of the peoples they conquered, being for the most part content simply to draw tribute from the conquered without making an effort to impose their own ways and ideas on them. Others, however, tried to stamp out the indigenous religion and culture by edict, mass slaughter, or even by transporting the entire population to a distant country.

*The wisdom and magnanimity of Alexander were on this occasion specifically evinced. He received in a friendly manner the proffered submission of the Jews, and showed the greatest deference to their religious scruples.*
—CLAUDE REIGNIER CONDER
on Alexander the Great
conquering Palestine

---

**Alexander the Great (356–323 B.C.) conquered most of the known world in less than 13 years. By establishing Greek language and culture alongside those of native peoples, he brought into being a new cosmopolitan culture, Hellenism, which linked the eastern and western worlds for centuries.**

But Alexander was of neither type. As he founded cities throughout his vast empire, he installed Greek officials to rule, administer, and develop his new territories, and set up Greek garrisons to defend against invasion or rebellion. With the establishment of Greek control came the promulgation of Greek culture, or Hellenism, throughout much of the known world. But Greek culture was not imposed at the expense of indigenous ways of life. Instead, it was intended to flourish side by side with already existing cultures as Alexander pursued his dream of uniting and melding the eastern and western worlds into one worldwide, cosmopolitan culture. Alexander often appointed the kings whom he defeated to administer the territory they had just lost, and he treated the armies he defeated with the same magnanimity, inviting them to join his army. Alexander, who himself adopted the ways of the Persian Empire he conquered, further fostered the merging of cultures by encouraging intermarriage and by appointing Greeks and non-Greeks to serve alongside each other in both administrative and military positions.

The city-states of Greece at that time were playing host to a remarkable flowering of literary, philosophic, and artistic expression. Alexander, who as an adolescent had been a student of the Greek philosopher Aristotle, spread these ideas across the eastern half of the known world; for example, Alexandria, a city he founded in Egypt, became the world center of scholarship for hundreds of years. Throughout the empire, Greek language and culture became the common bonds linking regions that until then had been vastly disparate. Thus in Palestine, to which Alexander granted limited self-government after occupying it in 332 B.C., Jewish religion and culture first came under the influence of Greek thought.

Upon Alexander's death in 323 B.C., the various territories of his empire were placed under the control of his leading generals. But wars immediately broke out between the generals, who eventually declared themselves kings of the territories they had

been assigned to administer. In 321 B.C., the 33-year-old Greek general Seleucus was rewarded for his role in the assassination of another general by being given control of Babylonia. He was soon driven out by rival generals, but in 312 B.C. he regained control of the region. By 285 B.C., he had conquered most of Alexander's old empire for himself, excluding Egypt and its province of Palestine. In the province of Syria, immediately north of Palestine, Seleucus founded the city of Antioch to serve as the capital of his empire.

Seleucus was assassinated in 280 B.C. The name of the empire he founded, Seleucid, is derived from his name. The Seleucids, whose capital was in Syria and whose roots were in Greece, are often referred to as Greco-Syrians. For the next century and a half they would control most of what is today known as the Middle East.

In 301 B.C., while Seleucus was building his own empire, Palestine was conquered by Egypt, which was ruled by another successor to Alexander, a general named Ptolemy. The Egyptians, who had thoroughly embraced Hellenism, exercised rigid control over economic life in Palestine. But they allowed the Jews to worship as they pleased; indeed, the Jewish religion flourished under Egyptian rule. According to one legend, an Egyptian king paid for 72 Jewish scholars to travel from Jerusalem to Alexandria, the Egyptian capital, around 250 B.C. to translate the Torah into Greek. Historians now believe that the translators were in fact Egyptian Jews using Torah scrolls sent from Jerusalem. Nevertheless, their work was the first translation of the Jewish scriptures into another language, and it was done so that the large Jewish community of Alexandria — which was already so Hellenized that it spoke Greek but little Hebrew — could understand its religion's holy texts.

In 198 B.C., the Seleucids conquered Palestine, taking it away from Egypt. The majority of Jews in Jerusalem supported the Seleucids in the war between the Greco-Syrians and the Egyptians, and in response the Seleucids guaranteed them full religious freedom and even assisted in repairing the Temple. Nevertheless, almost 150 years after the death of Alexander the Great, the Seleucids were still committed to spreading Hellenism throughout their dominions — though again like Alexander, they

A 19th-century view of Antioch, once the capital of the Seleucid Empire, now a small city in Turkey. Founded in 300 B.C., it was built to resemble the cities of Greece; minarets, like those seen here, did not appear for another 1,000 years.

intended it to coexist with the indigenous Jewish culture.

Upon taking control of Palestine, the Seleucids found some Jews already influenced by Hellenism. Since the days of Alexander and under the rule of the Hellenized Egyptians, many Jews in Palestine, particularly those who lived in the cities, had adopted Greek ways. As Seleucid rule became established and institutionalized within Palestine, the wealth of the Seleucid Empire gave urban Jews the leisure time to attend schools, theaters, and sporting events, all central features of Hellenistic life. New cities styled along Greek lines were built, and traditionally Jewish cities began to assume more of a Hellenistic character as Greek-style public buildings were put up, Greco-Syrian administrators took office, and garrisons of Seleucid soldiers settled in.

Less than 20 years after the Seleucids conquered Palestine, several "Greek" cities had been established throughout the country. According to the biblical historian D. S. Russell:

> Such cities are called "Greek," not in the sense that they were necessarily populated by native Greeks, but rather in the sense that they were organized according to a Greek pattern; for the most part they were inhabited by local people whose political and social life had undergone a complete reorientation. As such these cities were much more than merely "symbols" of the Greek way of life; they were living embodiments of it, demonstrating a civilization and culture unlike anything known there before. The method of government by democratic senate, for example . . . would no doubt give to the people an entirely new mental outlook. . . . [There] were educational institutions in which the young men of the day could gain an appreciation not only of literature and poetry and music but also of physical culture, which was of the very essence of Greek civilization. "They expressed," writes historian Edward Bevan, "fundamental tendencies of the Greek mind — its craving for harmonious beauty of form, its delight in the body, its unabashed frankness with regard to everything natural."

*The attitude of Hellenistic powers toward the religious customs and beliefs of particular ethnic groups was usually one of tolerance. Hellenism triumphed over national religions by infiltration and assimilation rather than by frontal attack or persecution.*
—WILLIAM REUBEN FARMER
American historian

As Hellenistic culture spread through the eastern world, the establishment of Greek institutions came with it. Theaters like the one shown here, schools, and gymnasiums, all central to Hellenistic life, were built in Judea. Many Jews embraced Hellenism.

The inhabitants of these "Greek" cities adopted Greek styles of dress, learned to speak Greek, and studied science and philosophy. Greek art and sculpture, with its remarkable depictions of the human form, appeared in all the cities. Greek institutions were established even in Jerusalem itself, as members of the Jewish upper class, those who aspired to improve their social or financial standing, and those who genuinely believed in the principles of the new culture began to embrace

Hellenism. "New aesthetic horizons had been opened up before the Jews in Jerusalem" writes Russell; "old Jewish customs and rites now appeared all too crude when judged by the standards of the 'new enlightenment.' "

As the Hellenistic way of life spread, some Jews adopted along with it the worship of Greek, Persian, Babylonian, or Egyptian deities, any or all of which were accepted as manifestations of divinity in Hellenistic belief. According to mainstream Hellenistic thought, all the peoples of the earth believed in the same divine spirit, no matter what names it was called by. The Greek Zeus or Athena, the Babylonian Ishtar or Enki, the Egyptian Ra or Isis, or the one god of the Jews — all were seen by the Hellenists as different names for the same divine spirit. Some Jews accepted this belief and recognized other gods in conjunction with their practice of Judaism.

At the foundations of Hellenistic religious beliefs stood the ancient gods of Greece: Zeus, king and most powerful of the gods; his wife, Hera; Athena, goddess of wisdom; Ares, god of war; Apollo, god of poetry and music; Dionysus, god of wine and ecstasy; Aphrodite, goddess of love and sexuality; and a host of other gods and mortals that composed the huge and rich pantheon of Greek mythology. An empire, a city, a family, or an individual would choose one or more of these gods to honor, in exchange, it was hoped, for the god's protection. But the worship of Greek gods was considered by most as the symbolic worship of other, more universal values. This is one of the reasons why Hellenistic culture so easily adopted the worship of foreign deities, which the Hellenes believed were symbolic of the same universal values.

More fundamental to Hellenistic belief than the worship of the gods, at least among the middle and upper classes, was the pursuit of perfection through the attainment of knowledge and wisdom. By following the established methods of striving for perfection in mind and body, each individual performed what to the Hellenes was a sacred task. The study of nature, philosophy, mathematics, his-

> *The true Hellenizers among the Jews were to be found in the ranks of the ruling aristocracy in Jerusalem. . . . The new culture, on its external side at any rate, implied a certain social standing, which was apparently more important to such people than religious scruples.*
> —D. S. RUSSELL

tory, drama, music, rhetoric, foreign cultures, and other subjects honed the mind and brought it into harmony with the world. Just as important was the pursuit of perfection in the body, and the well-rounded Hellene male was expected to excel at wrestling, running, discus and javelin throwing, and other forms of athletics. The human body itself was considered sacred; thus the Hellenes viewed the age-old Jewish practice of circumcision (the cutting of the foreskin among all males as a mark of Judaism) as a mutilation of the human body and therefore a barbaric sacrilege.

Many of the important gods in traditional Greek religion — and in Egyptian, Babylonian, and most other religions as well — were female, embodying qualities that later western cultures would not nec-

Hellenistic culture prized both physical and intellectual development, a concept often expressed in remarkable likenesses of the human form, such as this sculpture, The Discus Thrower. Traditional Judaism, however, regarded any depiction of the human form as blasphemous.

essarily attribute to women. The Greeks, for example, identified wisdom with Athena and hunting with Diana; later, an Egyptian belief was adopted and transformed into a cult worshiping a supreme deity known as the Great Mother of the Gods. It is not altogether surprising, therefore, that women in Hellenistic society enjoyed more freedom than in any previous society of the ancient world. The upper-class Hellene woman was encouraged to study many of the intellectual and artistic disciplines, could acquire wealth, and was able to mix freely with men — all of which stood in marked contrast to the status of women at even the highest levels of Jewish society. Still, the Hellene woman was not allowed to become a citizen, a privilege reserved for only a small percentage of the male population. Indeed, throughout the Hellenistic world, most men and women lived simply as farmers, herders, laborers, or merchants. Slavery was accepted as a fact, as it always had been, although under Hellenism it was possible for a slave to gain his or her freedom.

It was under Hellenism that the first doubts about the morality of slavery materialized, raised by a group of philosophers called the Stoics. Their teach-

Antiochus III (223—187 B.C.) wrested Palestine from the Egyptians in 198 B.C. Supported by most Jews during the war, he granted them full religious freedom. In 190 B.C., the Romans defeated him at the Battle of Magnesia in Turkey, forcing the Seleucids to pay Rome a huge tribute during the next several decades.

ings and those of several other groups of philosophers — all of which sought to guide the individual to peace, ethical justice, and moral rectitude — gained broad recognition and acceptance throughout the Hellenistic world. For many, the adherence to philosophic principles replaced the worship of gods as their central spiritual belief. Stoicism, founded by a Hellenized Phoenician named Zeno, was the most widely followed philosophy. According to the historian V. L. Ehrenberg, Stoicism taught that "there was no difference between Greek and non-Greek, man and woman, free and slave. The great idea of the brotherhood of men originated from the Stoics."

But in spite of the teachings of the Stoics and the other advancements of Greek civilization, equality among people was an illusion in the Hellenistic world. Native Greeks held most of the positions of control in the military, economic, and governmental administration; the only non-Greeks to hold such positions were those locals who in effect had become Greek by fully embracing Hellenism. The Hellenists tended to regard most local religions and customs as barbaric, accepting such beliefs only after they had been processed through the filter of Greek ideas. Thus when the majority of Jews proved unwilling to compromise their religion, the Seleucids responded with great brutality to what they regarded as the stubbornness of a backward, inferior people.

The malleability of the Hellenistic belief in the gods, besides leading to the acceptance of foreign gods, also led to the phenomenon of emperor worship. Alexander the Great, for example, successfully petitioned the Greek religious authorities for the right to be worshiped as a living god. Subsequent Seleucid emperors also declared themselves gods, a practice common among the Babylonians, Persians, Egyptians, and other eastern peoples. Antiochus IV, who took the name "Epiphanes" ("God made manifest"), was no exception; the statues of Zeus he ordered to be erected and worshiped in Palestine bore his image. The refusal by most Jews to pay homage to Antiochus IV's divinity as other peoples had done was seen by the Greco-Syrians as an arrogant affront to their authority.

Hellenism was accepted and embraced by many among the Jewish upper and middle classes, but the peasantry and other more conservative and religious elements in Jewish society opposed it. They saw it not only as antithetical to Jewish beliefs and a threat to Jewish identity, but more importantly, as sacrilegious. The worship of other gods was considered an abomination and a threat to the actual lives and existence of the Jewish people. The Jews, who believed that any painting, drawing, mosaic, or statue of the human or animal form was idolatry (the worship of idols), saw the Greeks' art, with its depictions of humans and animals in scenes from mythology, legend, and everyday life, as a blasphemous violation of God's law. Greek religion regarded the pig as a sacred symbol of fertility, but Jewish law forbade the eating or even the touching of any part of a pig. In ritual, customs, modes of conduct, and many other cultural aspects, Hellenism and Judaism were diametrically opposed to each other.

Around 180 B.C., the Hasidim — literally, "the Pious" — were recognized as an organized group within Judaism that was strongly opposed to Hellenism, though they were not yet willing to take up arms against the Greco-Syrians. They and other Jews formed a strong anti-Seleucid bloc that often supported the Egyptians, the enemies of the Seleucids.

Antiochus IV Epiphanes seized power as king of the Seleucid Empire in 176 B.C. He had spent 12 years of his life as a hostage in Rome under terms of a treaty the empire had been forced to sign in 190 B.C., after the Romans had crushed Seleucid forces in the Battle of Magnesia. The Magnesia treaty stipulated that the Seleucids had to pay a huge tribute to Rome in periodic installments and were required to hand over more than 20 prominent people as hostages to guarantee Seleucid compliance with the treaty terms. After he was released by the Romans, Antiochus stayed in Athens, where he

Antiochus IV seized the Seleucid throne in 176 B.C. after spending years as a hostage in Rome under terms of the Magnesia treaty. In 170 B.C. he ordered his subjects to worship him as a god; three years later he handed down the anti-Jewish decrees, in part to impose discipline on his empire's southernmost outpost.

learned that his brother, the king, had been murdered and that his young nephew was the new king. He arrived in Antioch, staged a coup d'état, executed his nephew, and took over the throne.

Throughout most of his realm, Antiochus IV continued the policy of religious tolerance that his predecessors had followed. In addition to Hellenism's natural tolerance for other religions, there were political reasons for Antiochus IV to allow the practice of local religions. The Seleucid Empire was under pressure from the Romans to the west, the Parthians to the east, and the Egyptians to the south. In order to guarantee the loyalty of conquered states, Antiochus IV tolerated and even supported the practice of local religions. In Babylonia, for example, he revived that nation's ancient religion in an effort to secure the support of that province's population. Even after he ordered the worship of himself as an incarnation of Zeus throughout the empire in about 169 B.C., he still continued to tolerate and support indigenous religions.

But within one year's time, Antiochus IV outlawed traditional Judaism. His anti-Jewish decrees were a complete reversal of the Seleucids' 30-year policy of tolerance toward Judaism. Why did Antiochus IV single out Judaism for suppression?

Judea was the southernmost outpost of the Seleucid Empire. The Egyptians were a major threat to the Seleucids, and Antiochus IV correctly suspected orthodox Jews of supporting his archrivals in the area, the Egyptians. As biblical historian H. A. Fischel writes, "The existence [in Judea] of a pro-Egyptian party . . . and [Judea's] strategical importance as a border province aggravated an already precarious situation." The stage was set for a clash between the Seleucids and their Hellenized supporters among the Jewish aristocracy on the one hand, and the religious Jews supporting the Egyptians on the other.

That clash occurred in 169 B.C., when fighting broke out in Jerusalem between forces supporting Jason and Menelaus, two pro-Hellenist rivals for the office of high priest. Menelaus was Antiochus IV's man; he had stripped the Temple to pay bribes to

> *Inherent in Hellenism was an inexorable challenge to the particularity of the Torah.*
> —WILLIAM REUBEN FARMER
> American historian

the king and was despised by the orthodox Jews. Jason — the king's previous appointee who had been outbribed for the job by Menelaus — was likewise despised by the majority of the population. Jason emerged victorious and proceeded to slaughter hundreds of the city's inhabitants.

Later in 169 B.C., Antiochus IV, returning from a successful military campaign in Egypt, heard of Jason's seizure of the high priesthood and the resulting chaos in his empire's southernmost citadel. Antiochus IV responded ruthlessly to the coup. He and his army entered Jerusalem, reinstated Menelaus, and slaughtered the inhabitants. He then sacked the Temple, using the gold and treasures he took to pay off the Romans, to whom the empire owed another tribute payment as stipulated by the

A Jewish priest of the Maccabean era as depicted in a 19th-century illustration. Under Seleucid rule, the leading priests were appointed by the king; under Antiochus IV, they supported the anti-Jewish decrees, presided over the worship of Zeus, and even participated in the looting of the Temple.

A 15th-century French illustration depicting the occupation of Jerusalem and the looting of the Temple by Seleucid forces in 168 B.C. Antiochus IV plundered shrines throughout his empire, using the loot to pay the huge Roman tribute and to finance his armies.

Magnesia treaty. Having shown that he would brook no challenge to his authority, Antiochus IV withdrew.

One year later, Antiochus IV mounted a second campaign against Egypt in an attempt to crush it for good. But with the Seleucids on the verge of complete victory, the Roman Empire threatened to intervene and Antiochus IV was forced to withdraw in humiliation. As he returned from his setback in Egypt, Antiochus IV appointed Apollonius, already the chief minister of finance, to be governor of Palestine. The infuriated king then ordered him to sack Jerusalem. Apollonius split off from the main imperial force with a large detachment of mercenaries and waited outside the city walls until the Sabbath, when the Jews would not defend themselves. He then rushed through the gates, sacked the entire city, massacred its inhabitants, and pulled down the city walls, leaving Jerusalem wrecked, depopulated, and defenseless.

Apollonius then built the Acra to secure the empire's hold over Jerusalem and to provide a bulwark against any possible Egyptian encroachments from the south. Perhaps even more important, the Acra served to keep religious, potentially pro-Egyptian Jews from returning to their most sacred place, the Temple, thus denying them a symbolic rallying point for rebellion against Seleucid rule.

The Temple was now used by Syrian soldiers to worship the god Baal Shamen ("Lord of Heaven"). By the beginning of 167 B.C., Antiochus IV's anti-Jewish decrees went into effect. Torahs were burned, circumcision was outlawed, observance of Jewish holidays and the Sabbath was banned, and Jews throughout the province were ordered to worship the gods of the Seleucids — all with the collaboration of Menelaus and the Hellenized Jews. At the end of 167 B.C., Antiochus IV rededicated the Jerusalem Temple as a shrine to Zeus.

The Greco-Syrians were now at war with the majority of the Jewish population.

*It cannot be emphasized too strongly that such extreme forms of opposition to the Jewish Torah [e.g. eating pork] on the part of the heathen are only found to characterize the final stage of the conflict between Hellenism and Judaism.*
—WILLIAM REUBEN FARMER
American historian

**37**

# 3

# The Jews and Judaism

Unquestionably the principal motivation for the ferocious resistance put up by the Jews against the Seleucids in the Maccabean revolt was the Jews' intense devotion to their religion. Long before the Maccabean revolt, Judaism had already survived several threats to its existence.

Historians and archaeologists, after years of studying Biblical texts along with artifacts, ruins, and documents from other ancient cultures, now believe that Judaism was founded sometime around 1750 B.C. According to the Torah, the founder was Abraham, a Hebrew tribesman who lived in Ur (located in present-day Iraq), a great city that was the center of the Sumerian Empire, predecessor to the Babylonian and Persian empires. According to the Torah, God told Abraham to leave Ur and travel south, whcrc hc would find a rich land that would serve as a home to Abraham, his clan, and his descendants. Many historians believe that Abraham's one god was actually his family god or household god; archaeologists have found that every home in Ur contained a shrine where a family's personal protective deities were worshiped. At any rate, during

*Jewish nationalism throughout the Hellenistic period is characterized by "zeal for the Torah." Behind this zeal for the Law lay the more fundamental and original zeal for the covenant [with the] God of Israel.*
—WILLIAM REUBEN FARMER
American historian

**Moses descends Mount Sinai and brings the Law to the Jewish people. Moses appears, as described in the book of Exodus, with two rays of light emanating from his head. The event is said to have occurred after the Hebrew tribes left Egypt, which historians date at about 1250 B.C.**

the next few hundred years, the Hebrew clans eventually found their way to Palestine. There they continued to live as herdsmen alongside the original, settled inhabitants, the Canaanites, and intermarried with them.

The concept of one and only one god ruling the universe—monotheism—was what set the Hebrews apart from their neighbors. Though there are signs that the early Hebrews' beliefs contained some elements of polytheism (the belief in several gods) and that other peoples practiced forms of monotheism — notably the Sumerians and Canaanites — it appears that the Hebrews were the only people who believed in a single, all-encompassing deity.

**The prophet Nehemiah oversees the building of the Second Temple about 515 B.C. The First Temple, built by King Solomon around 950 B.C., was destroyed 4 centuries later by the Babylonians.**

Around 1370 B.C., many of the seminomadic Hebrew tribes migrated to Egypt, which was ruled by the powerful pharaoh Ramses II. At first free and prosperous in Egypt, the Hebrews were later subjugated and enslaved. By about 1250 B.C., they were allowed to emigrate from Egypt, led, according to the Torah, by Moses. There followed what the Bible describes as 40 years of wandering in the Sinai desert. According to the Bible, it was during these wanderings that Moses received the foundations of the Torah — the detailed body of Jewish history, law, and code of worship — from God. The covenant between God and the Hebrews was renewed. They believed that God had delivered them from slavery and promised to return them to their land; in exchange, they were strictly bound to follow his commandments — the Law — and to worship him and him alone. The Hebrew tribes now regarded themselves as the nation of Israel, God's chosen people.

Just after Moses's death, the 12 Israelite tribes united and conquered Canaan, the land of their ancestors. By 1000 B.C. they had established a powerful nation, Israel, by conquering the other nations of Palestine. Under their kings Saul, David, and Solomon, many of the conquered converted to Judaism, either voluntarily or by means of force. During his reign, David captured the already ancient Canaanite city of Jerusalem, and made it his capital. His successor, King Solomon, built the Temple around 950 B.C., and the highly ritualized worship of God and the Law was instituted, closely managed and safeguarded by a class of high priests.

Upon the death of Solomon in 922 B.C., the kingdom was split in half. The northern half was called Israel and its capital, Samaria; the southern half was called Judah and its capital, Jerusalem. Israel soon recognized the worship of other deities, though it still regarded God as supreme. In 721 B.C. Israel was conquered by the Assyrian Empire and ceased to exist. The people of Judah believed that the kingdom of Israel fell because it violated God's covenant by worshiping other gods.

The Assyrians conquered the kingdom of Judah as well. Around 680 B.C., the worship of Assyrian

*The land of Canaan had been promised to Abraham. It was this promise which sustained the Israelites during their forty-year sojourn in the wilderness. It emboldened them in their conquest of Canaan under Joshua, and later it strengthened them in their resistance to the incursions of the Philistines.*
—CLAUDE REIGNIER CONDER
British historian

gods alongside that of the Jewish god was begun. Fifty years later Judah regained its independence, but religious Jews viewed the worship of Assyrian gods on Jewish soil as another violation of the covenant with God.

In 597 B.C., the Babylonian Empire, which had succeeded the Assyrians as the superpower of the age, conquered Judah and Jerusalem and took many Jews to Babylon as captives. In response to a rebellion 10 years later, the Babylonians returned and destroyed Jerusalem, massacred all its political and religious officials, burned the Temple to the ground and destroyed its walls, and carried away the population of the wrecked city and surrounding area to Babylon. Other Jews fled to Egypt. The kingdom of Judah was no more. The disastrous fall of Jerusalem was the turning point in the people's history and would continue to be regarded as such for several hundred years.

The Babylonian exile lasted 50 years, during which time, according to Jewish legend, at least one unsuccessful attempt was made to wipe out the Jews living in Babylon. By 537 B.C., the Babylonians were themselves conquered by the Persian Empire, and some Jews were allowed to return to Palestine. Jerusalem and its Temple were rebuilt by 515 B.C., but it was little more than a remote, thinly populated outpost. Many Jews preferred to remain in Babylon under Persian rule, where a large and important Jewish community developed.

The Jews who returned to Jerusalem, believing that the fall of Judah had been caused by the worship of other gods in God's holy land, expelled all non-Jews from the city and surrounding countryside. This would ensure that there was no threat that the Jews would abandon the Law and lapse into the worship of foreign gods. As the newly repopulated Jewish homeland slowly regained its vigor, the experiences of the disastrous events leading to the Babylonian exile created in the Jewish people a new piety and a far greater devotion to their god than had existed before.

The Torah and Temple were now the focus of Jewish existence. The entire nation was involved in ob-

*Neither famine, pestilence, nor incredible battle casualties could deter the Jews from their apparently insane refusal to surrender. But the moment the temple was set aflame . . . the defense of the city collapsed.*
—WILLIAM REUBEN FARMER
on the destruction of
the Temple

serving the word of the Law and fulfilling the obligations of Temple ritual. To ensure that both were carried out exactly as mandated, to be certain that the Jewish people made good on their half of the covenant with God, the high-priest class became the guardians of the religion. There were no kings; the high priest stood as the highest authority in the interpretation of the Law, both in worship at the Temple and in affairs of state. The nation had become an entirely religious entity, within which matters of religion and state were inseparable — and indeed, all political affairs were conducted in strict accordance with the dictates of religion.

The Temple ritual directed by the hierarchy of priests and subpriests was immensely intricate. There was a detailed calendar of feast days, days of fasting, sabbaths, and other holy days, each with its own special code of observances. On each day that was not a holy day, there were still two animal

**The ruins of a synagogue built in the Greek style. The Temple was the focus of Jewish ritual, but the synagogues (places of congregation) were where Jews throughout Judea and the rest of the world met to worship. Local synagogues were first established after the destruction of the First Temple by the Babylonians.**

sacrifices to perform, blessings to confer upon worshipers, and other rituals requiring prayers, chanting, choirs, orchestras, processions, and, of course, readings from the Torah. Men who lived in or near Jerusalem were required to be present at Temple ceremonies for a certain number of days, and those who lived too far away were required to participate in the prescribed rituals at local synagogues. In this way, every male member of the population took part in the worship of God during the course of each year.

In keeping with the high priest's position as head of state and the Temple's function as center of all aspects of national life, the outer portions of the Temple complex also served as palace and treasury. The complex was surrounded by a series of walls to prevent invaders from capturing or destroying the Temple as the Babylonians had done.

Meanwhile, the Torah itself was copied and distributed throughout the land in its original Hebrew. But by this time most of the population spoke Aramaic, a language closely related to Hebrew that was spoken throughout much of the Middle East. A class of translators called lay (nonpriestly) scribes came into being. They were charged with the task of making the Torah accessible to the majority of the population through translating, teaching, and interpreting. Whereas the high priests increasingly concerned themselves with Temple ritual and the management of power, the work of the lay scribes helped cement the devotion of the common people to the Torah—a devotion that would be dramatically demonstrated during the Maccabean revolt.

Another factor that contributed to the intensity of the Maccabean revolt was the influence of Babylonian religion on Judaism. During the Jews' exile in Babylon, certain ideas springing from the Torah were transformed. For example, the concept of angels, present in the Torah, and the later concept of demons, were modified through contact with Babylonian beliefs. By the time of the Maccabees, Jews believed in a hierarchy of angels and demons and that the angels would fight and triumph alongside

*Twice every year every male Jew was commanded to visit Jerusalem, and the organisation by which this duty was carried out formed a fundamental part of the individual and national life.*
—CLAUDE REIGNIER CONDER
on early Judaism

the righteous in defense of the Law. This belief may have been a factor in the Maccabean rebels' great courage in the face of overwhelming odds. In 2 Maccabees, the second of two books of the period that recount the Maccabean revolt, accounts of the rebels' victories over the Seleucids are accompanied by descriptions of angelic armies preceding the Maccabees into battle.

The Jews also adopted from Babylonian religion the concept of an inevitable, final, all-consuming battle between good and evil in which huge numbers of the righteous would fall before good would finally prevail, and the concept of resurrection, in which the righteous would be raised from the dead and live in a kingdom of God on earth. These two beliefs may have provided the Maccabean rebels with further encouragement to fight and die willingly for the Law.

The Law for which the Jewish rebels fought and died was more than 1,000 years old by the time of the Maccabean revolt. Biblical historians believe that the Torah was originally a set of ancient oral traditions stretching back to the time of Abraham, and archaeological research in this century has corroborated some historical events described in the Torah that actually did occur around 1800 B.C. Historians date the writing down of these laws and traditions in the Torah as occurring in several stages between 1000 B.C. and 350 B.C., although they agree that it may indeed have appeared as a written work long before then.

The Torah comprises the Five Books of Moses: Genesis, the story of the creation of the world to the Hebrews' arrival in Egypt; Exodus, the story of their subjugation and flight from Egypt to Moses' being given the Law on Mount Sinai; Leviticus, a collection of laws; Numbers, an account of the Hebrews' wandering in the desert; and Deuteronomy, another collection of laws that includes an account of the death of Moses. Biblical scholars have been able to sort out within these five books a number of different narrative strands, indicating that the writing of the books spanned several different eras. Some of

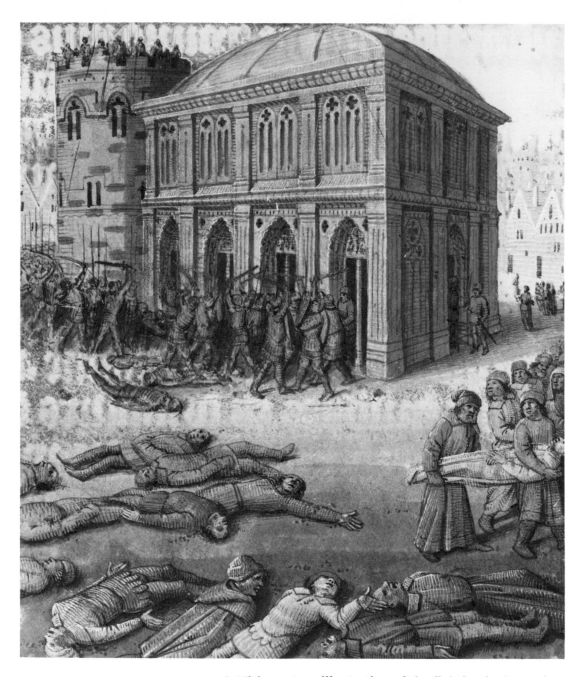

A 15th-century illustration of the fighting in Jerusalem
between the forces of Jason and Menelaus, two Hellenist
rivals for the office of high priest. Antiochus IV in-
terceded in favor of Menelaus; to support him and
strengthen the Seleucids' grip on Judea, Antiochus IV
built the Acra fortress alongside the Temple.

the traditions found in the Torah appear to stretch back to 1800 B.C. and earlier, whereas others date from about 350 B.C. There are also indications that some of the narrative is a product of traditions from the northern Hebrew tribes, and others come from southern tribal traditions.

During the Maccabean period, the high priests of the Temple regarded the Torah as the religion's only sacred book. The Hasidim and lay scribes also regarded as sacred the books of the prophets (Joshua, Judges, 1 and 2 Samuel, 1 and 2 Kings, and several books of the minor prophets). Like the Torah, these were written in many stages during a period that spanned several different eras. Part of 2 Samuel was written in 1000 B.C. (historians believe it is the oldest written portion of the Bible to be preserved in its original form); the latest was written by 200 B.C. The books of the prophets covered Jewish history up to the Babylonian exile. Other later writings — some of which are part of the Jewish Bible today, some of which are not — were also considered sacred. But at no time was any book or writing held in such high esteem among all Jews as the Torah.

All these currents in Jewish history played key roles in the Maccabean revolt. The revolt was not so much a struggle for political independence as we think of it today, but rather a war fought to guarantee that the Jewish people could worship their god in accordance with the ancient dictates of their religion. When Judah Maccabee asked his fellow Jews to fight alongside him, he always appealed to their zeal for the Torah and their obligation to uphold the covenant between the Jewish people and their god.

The Torah — also known as the Five Books of Moses or, simply, the Law — is the foundation of Judaism. It contains the wisdom, laws, and commandments that govern the Jewish people; according to Jewish tradition, much of it was given directly by God to Moses.

# 4

# The Revolt

Nothing is recorded about Judah Maccabee's early life except that he was one of the five sons of Mattathias, a priest who had once lived in Jerusalem, and that they all lived in the village of Modin. Judah was able to follow events in the Temple because his father, Mattathias, from the tribal family of Hashmon, served in his priestly duties there at least four weeks a year.

Early in 167 B.C., after Antiochus IV had reestablished Menelaus as high priest of the Temple, the enforcement of Hellenization in Judea was begun. Imperial soldiers spread out from Jerusalem to compel the observance of the Hellenization decrees, which effectively abolished the Jewish religion. In every village, Jews were forced to build altars and make animal sacrifices to Zeus and to participate in the worship of Antiochus IV, who was himself identified with Zeus. Torahs were burned, Jews were not allowed to keep the Sabbath, and the circumcision of male infants, which under Jewish law was to be performed when the baby was eight days old, was forbidden. The penalty for violating the Hellenization decrees was torture and death.

*Although they [the Jews] were tortured and distorted, burnt and torn to pieces, and went through all kinds of instruments of torture, that they might be forced either to blaspheme their legislator, or to eat what was forbidden them, yet could they not be made to do either.*
—JOSEPHUS
Roman historian

**An illustration from a 10th-century Bible depicting the start of the Maccabean revolt. At center, Mattathias kills the Jew who had agreed to sacrifice a pig to Zeus. At top, one of Mattathias's five sons kills a Seleucid soldier sent to enforce the anti-Jewish decrees.**

Antiochus IV banned upon penalty of death the age-old rite of circumcision, in which Jews cut the foreskin of their male infants to identify them as Jews. He held the Hellenistic view that any such alteration of the human body was mutilation. This illustration is from a 13th-century Torah.

What happened next in the village of Modin is recorded in 1 and 2 Maccabees. Historians believe that 1 Maccabees was written sometime between 135 B.C. and 110 B.C., 25 to 50 years after the Maccabean revolt, by a Judean who may well have been an eyewitness to several of the events he describes. Although the author was a pious Jew writing in Hebrew and concerned that his people pay proper reverence to God and the Torah, his book is first and foremost a history that very rarely makes reference to theology. It is considered to be by far the most accurate account of the Maccabean period.

Historians believe that 2 Maccabees was written later, between 100 B.C. and 50 B.C., by a Jew who lived outside Palestine, perhaps in Alexandria. It was written in Greek and is apparently an abridgment of a much longer book that has since been lost. The author of 2 Maccabees, who includes several passages involving angels and miracles and omits some unflattering information about the Maccabees, is less concerned with accurate history than he is with telling a story that illustrates the concept of God's deliverance of his people.

Other accounts written by historians during the 200 years following the Maccabean revolt — particularly the works of Flavius Josephus, a Jewish historian who wrote during the height of the Roman Empire — and the records of the Seleucid Empire itself provide the rest of the story that has come down to us today.

A Seleucid official named Apelles and his detachment of imperial soldiers arrived in Modin one morning late in 167 B.C. They built a stone altar in the market square and lifted a totem to Zeus above it. Everyone was ordered to dress for worship and meet in the square by noon for the sacrifice decreed by Antiochus IV.

The sun was high overhead when the villagers, hushed and waiting, gathered in the marketplace. Judah's father, the priest Mattathias, stood in front of the villagers, his *tallith* (a white-fringed prayer shawl with tassels on the four corners) drawn over his head. Judah and his four brothers, John, Simon, Eleazar, and Jonathan, stood behind their father. On the other side of the market square stood Apelles and his soldiers. Between the two groups stood the altar to Zeus and, tethered to it, a pig — both shockingly pagan symbols to the Jewish villagers.

A Doré illustration depicts the aged priest Mattathias, Judah Maccabee's father, killing a Jew who was disloyal to the faith in the village of Modin. The incident, according to 1 Maccabees, started the Maccabean revolt. Mattathias was recognized as the leader of the insurrection.

The soldiers must have leaned on their spears and yawned. This was just one village in a series of many. The Seleucids had ways of dealing with the Jews who refused to take part in the sacrifice. In 2 Maccabees there are two stories that tell of the tortures inflicted on recalcitrant Jews; although both are considered legends, scholars believe they are based on actual incidents.

An old man of 90 named Eleazar refused to eat the swine sacrificed to Zeus and was whipped almost to death. Then the soldiers stopped and offered to let him live if he would just act as though he had eaten of the sacrifice; he could substitute any meat he chose. He refused and said, "I leave to the young a noble example of how to go eagerly and nobly to die a beautiful death in the defense of our reverend and sacred laws." The angry soldiers finished whipping him to death.

The second story is of a mother and her seven sons who also refused to participate in a pagan sacrifice and were brought before Antiochus IV. Starting with the oldest son and on down to the youngest, each in turn was tortured, mutilated, and killed

**Antiochus IV's Hellenization decrees abolished the Jewish religion, prescribing the death penalty for all Jews who failed to pay homage to Zeus and the Seleucid king. A story in 2 Maccabees tells of the 90-year-old scribe Eleazar, who chose to be tortured to death rather than abide by the king's decrees.**

after refusing to take part in the sacrifice. "And last, after her sons, died the mother."

By the time Apelles arrived in Modin, many Jews in the province already had died in defiance of the king's decree. Many others had fled. But none had risen up in revolt. That was about to change.

Apelles stepped forward next to the altar and spoke loudly for all in the village square to hear, challenging Mattathias to be the first to come forward and obey the King.

Mattathias refused, nor did Judah or any of his brothers step forward to help with the sacrifice.

Apelles, prepared for this defiance, took a large purple cloak and floppy purple hat, both symbols of priestly rank among the Seleucids, from one of the soldiers and lifted them for Mattathias to take. "Be the first to come forward and carry out the orders of the king; you and your sons will be raised to the rank of the Friends of the King . . . and given grants of silver and gold."

Mattathias stepped back and said, "I and my sons and my brethren walk in the covenant of our fathers. Heaven forbid that we should forsake the Law and the ordinances; the law of the king we will not obey by departing from our worship."

The soldiers looked at each other knowingly. It was time to make an example. Then the rest of the village would fall into line. They grabbed their spears, ready for the signal from their commander. Fathers and mothers drew their children close. Everyone waited for the violent climax to the confrontation.

At that moment, one of the villagers stepped forward and announced he would make the sacrifice and accept the king's rich offer. The soldiers relaxed. The apostate (a defector from a religion) lifted the squealing pig onto the altar and tied it down. Apelles handed him a *kopisin*, a butchering ax used for sacrifices. As the apostate lifted the ax over his head, Mattathias, in a rage, rushed forward and tore the ax from his grasp. He killed the apostate on the pagan altar, then turned on the astonished Apelles and slew him also. The villagers, led by Judah and his brothers, overwhelmed the surprised soldiers and killed them all.

Animal sacrifice was an important element of most ancient religions, including Judaism. Hellenistic ritual featured the sacrifice of pigs, animals regarded by Judaism as unclean; when Antiochus IV ordered the sacrificial offering of pigs to Zeus, the Jews refused.

After the incident at Modin, the villagers fled to the nearby Gophna hills, where Mattathias and his sons made their headquarters for the first stage of the revolt. Here Mattathias, near death, is shown asking Jewish refugees to be "zealous for the Law" and to be willing to "give your lives for the covenant of your fathers."

It all ended in minutes. The Jews had acted in passion rather than in a planned revolt, but what next? Apelles and his soldiers would be missed and a larger detachment of soldiers would surely come and burn the village to the ground.

But Judah, his father, and brothers had raised the flag of revolt in Judea — they had struck against the enemy and with the help of God would do so again. Certain of their own deaths, at least they would fight.

Mattathias called on his fellow Jews to do likewise. "Let everyone who is zealous for the Torah and would maintain the covenant, follow me."

During the night they stole away from their homes, careful to avoid any Seleucid soldiers patrolling the roads. Taking with them nothing more than their sheep, goats, and cattle, the villagers made their way to the steep wooded hills of Gophna, about nine miles northeast of Modin. In the Gophna hills they hoped to survive.

Judah was put in charge of the defenses. The first weeks at Gophna were critical. He prepared places around the rebel camp to ambush any attackers and put sentries to watch all approaches.

Once their position was secure, Judah and a few selected men moved out at night to the surrounding towns and villages and recruited men for the rebellion. Men who wanted to fight would come to Gophna for training. He organized an intelligence network, a supply system, and a messenger service that spread the news of the revolt.

Throughout Judea the Hasidim had fled from the Seleucid persecutions. Southeast of Jerusalem a large party of refugee Hasidim gathered in a cave. Seleucid soldiers found them and drew up in battle formation to attack. The soldiers shouted for them to come down from the cave and promised that their lives would be spared. It was the Sabbath, the day of rest ordered by Jewish law, and the Hasidim would not break the Sabbath even to save their lives. The soldiers attacked. The Hasidim would not defend themselves or even barricade the caves, because to do so would constitute a breach of the Law by performing work on the day of rest. All of them were killed, more than a thousand men, women, and children.

Mattathias, on hearing about the deaths of the Hasidim, made the decision that made the revolt possible: If attacked on the Sabbath, Jews would defend themselves. It was a revolutionary decision that guides the Jewish army of Israel even today. Nevertheless, this expedient choice was not accepted by all Jews. The account in 2 Maccabees, for example, omits references to the rebels fighting on the Sabbath, and there is evidence that later Jewish writings played down the Maccabees in part because of their decision to fight on the Sabbath.

The news that there was a group of Jews willing to fight the Seleucid army must have spread quickly. At that point, Jews who were hiding throughout Judea made their way to the Gophna hills to join the movement. The Hasidim threw the weight of their support behind the leadership of Mattathias, giving the revolt the broad-based manpower and support it needed to get under way in earnest.

Groups of a few armed rebels raided easy targets throughout Judea, attacking small, isolated Seleucid units. They also directed attacks against apostate Jews, slipping into villages at night, killing any apostates who supported the Seleucids, throwing down the altars to Zeus or Antiochus IV, and circumcising any male babies whose parents had followed the king's decree not to do so.

In the spring of 166 B.C., Mattathias, an old man, died. The leadership of the revolt now fell to his son Judah, surnamed Maccabee. Although there is evidence that the surname might be derived from words meaning "piercer" or "he who hides himself," it is generally assumed that the surname signifies "hammer" or "hammerer," from *maqqaba*, a word in Aramaic. The name Maccabee came to be applied to the whole revolt and its soldiers.

> *As for Judas Maccabeus, he hath been mighty and strong, even from his youth up: let him be your captain, and fight the battle of the people.*
> —MATTATHIAS
> Judah Maccabee's father, addressing his sons just before his death

נת ושכוד משום החין יויק
תתער הבה יתוער כרבב יון
חן זוחתה על הישי ויומרי
למות

מכבי

לברית ווחן לשום קטתה ירון ק

# 5

# Judah the Leader

In Judah Maccabee, the revolt found a leader with a rare combination of ruthlessness, righteousness, and brilliance in warfare. He ordered actions, such as the traditional Jewish practice of circumcising male babies, that would certainly bring reprisals on his own people. He possessed an unshakable belief that God was with him. He directed the war like a skilled veteran, devising strategies that suited the countryside where he fought. A thoughtful tactician, he was daring, but never careless. He learned quickly from his mistakes and demonstrated ability in the whole spectrum of military activity, from small raiding parties involving a handful of soldiers to major battles involving thousands of men. In victory or defeat he always strategically advanced his cause for freedom.

With every raid, the rebels attracted new supporters who came to Gophna for military training. Throughout northern Judea villagers returned home trained for warfare. Judah was able to expand the scope of his operations against the Seleucid control of Judea.

*The Jews began to understand that a great deliverer had arisen, and they flocked to the camp of Judas.*
—CLAUDE REIGNIER CONDER
British historian

A brilliant military tactician who excelled in both guerrilla warfare and pitched battles, Judah was given the name "Maccabee" (hammerer) by the Jews. In this illustration from a medieval Hebrew Bible, Judah's shield is adorned by the lion of Judea.

Judea at this time was only one small portion of Palestine, the region that today comprises southern Lebanon, Israel, and the Israeli-occupied territories of the Gaza Strip and the West Bank of the Jordan River. The Judea of the Maccabean era was a roughly circular territory, no more than 30 miles across in any direction, with Jerusalem in the center. Immediately to the north stood another small territory, known as the Toparchies, that was politically attached to Judea and made up mostly of Jewish towns, including Modin. Surrounding these Jewish territories within Palestine were a number of non-Jewish territories: Idumaea, Nabataea, and Ammon to the south and east, inhabited by desert nomads and seminomads; Philistia and Phoenicia to the west on the coast, the latter an ancient seafaring nation that had specialized in international trade for more than 2,000 years; Samaria and Galilee to the north, both areas that had once been Jewish in a strict sense but by Maccabean times were enemies of the Judeans. Although Jews lived in all these regions of Palestine, only Judea was a Jewish territory. At first, Judah and his men would isolate a lone patrol of Seleucid soldiers and kill them, stripping the dead soldiers of weapons and armor and hiding the bodies. One patrol, then two, disappeared; when soldiers were sent out to search, they were also attacked and killed. Eventually, the Seleucid garrison at the Acra in Jerusalem, its supply of soldiers limited, stopped sending out patrols.

Next, Judah took control of the roads leading to Jerusalem. The Maccabees openly took charge of many villages in the north. Trade and communications between Seleucid-held Jerusalem and Antioch, the empire's capital, were severed, leaving the Acra isolated and its garrison increasingly desperate.

If a large force moved out from the Acra and tried to force open the roads, the Maccabees harassed them, picking off a few men at a time and finally forcing them to retreat to the Acra. The Acra commander put out a call for help to the province governor, Apollonius, in Samaria.

The Samaritans and Judeans had been enemies for hundreds of years, ever since 922 B.C., when, with the death of Solomon, the Jewish kingdom split into the northern kingdom of Israel, later known as Samaria, and the southern kingdom of Judah, later known as Judea. During the next 200 years, the two Jewish kingdoms fought often. When Israel-Samaria fell to the Assyrians in 721 B.C., much of the Samaritan population was carried away (thus the legend of the 10 Lost Tribes of Israel) and many Assyrian settlers moved in. The Jews of the south never again considered the Samaritans to be true Jews — even around 515 B.C., when the Samaritans offered to help the Judeans in rebuilding the Temple in Jerusalem. The Judeans refused, still regarding the Samaritans as having been too corrupted by idolatry and intermarriage to be true Jews. The old hostilities between the two regions were reestablished. In 332 B.C., the Samaritans built their own temple, where their worship, wholly Jewish but distinct from that of the Judeans, was based purely on the Torah.

The Samaritans, too, had been forbidden to practice their form of Judaism by Antiochus IV's Hellenization decrees. But in the early summer of 166 B.C., Apollonius moved to crush the revolt in Judea by raising an army that included many Samaritans. It is possible that the Seleucids offered to lessen the anti-Jewish measures in Samaria in return for Samaritan soldiers, and perhaps the Samaritans were happy to march against their old rivals in Judea. However, the histories are silent on these points.

Apollonius took his troops and marched the quickest way from Samaria to Jerusalem, on a road that led due south next to the Gophna hills. The army, though its size is not recorded in ancient records, may have numbered 3,000 or slightly more and was a provincial force, not made up of imperial troops. The Samaria-Jerusalem road along which the army traveled runs through several narrow gorges. One, which most historians believe to be the place of battle, is called the Ascent of Lebonah, where the road winds uphill for several miles.

Judah knew that the army was on the move from Samaria. As Apollonius neared the Ascent of Lebonah, Judah's patrols kept him informed of every movement the Seleucid army made.

With the enemy close at hand, Judah moved his soldiers, fewer than a thousand, out of the Gophna hills. They were poorly equipped compared to the Seleucid provincials, who had long spears and heavy armor, but they were determined and desperate.

Judah chose an ambush position that would make the battle take place late in the day, so that if his men were defeated, they could escape under the cover of darkness. He divided his army into three groups, one large and two smaller. The smaller groups, made up mostly of slingers (men with leather slings that threw deadly fist-sized stones) and archers, were stationed on either side of the gorge. At the end of the gorge he stood with the main portion of his army ready for combat.

The enemy moved along the road in four columns, the standard traveling formation for armies in those days. Skirmishers (lightly armed troops with bows and slings) moved in front of the army. These were followed by a phalanx of 1,000 heavily armed infantry. Apollonius rode with his cavalry in the center,

Judah's rout of Apollonius's forces took place here, at the Ascent of Lebonah, where the narrow road to Jerusalem winds uphill. Detailed accounts of this and several other battles were recorded by the Jewish historian Flavius Josephus, who wrote in the 1st century A.D.

and another phalanx of 1,000 heavy infantry followed. Light troops brought up the rear.

As the Seleucid soldiers neared the end of the gorge, Judah and his men leaped from their hiding places and drove the skirmishers back onto the main body of the army. Before they could organize into their phalanx battle position, the Maccabees attacked them. The main body of the enemy army packed together in confusion. The signal was sounded and the ambushers on either side of the gorge fired their arrows and stones point-blank into the mass of soldiers. On all sides the Maccabees pressed home the attack.

"Many [Gentiles] fell and the rest fled," reports 1 Maccabees. Apollonius was killed and his army defeated, the first victory of any magnitude for the rebels. "Judah took Apollonius's sword," according to the account, "and ever after used it in battle."

Jews throughout the country rejoiced at the news of the victory. New volunteers flocked to join the rebel forces, who now controlled the northern half of Judea. The Seleucid garrison in the Acra, the high priest Menelaus, and his Jewish Hellenistic collaborators were isolated in Jerusalem.

**The imperial and provincial troops of the Seleucid Empire wore and used Greek-style equipment: plumed helmets, long spears, short swords, bronze shields, and breastplates. The rider in the background wears the Hellenistic civilian dress of the period: cape, skirt, and round, wide-brimmed hat.**

Judah mortally wounds Apollonius, the Seleucid general. The first major engagement of the Maccabean revolt took place in the summer of 166 B.C., when Judah and his forces ambushed and destroyed a provincial army led by Apollonius. According to 1 Maccabees, "Judah took Apollonius's sword and ever after used it in battle."

In early autumn a larger Seleucid provincial army moved from the Phoenician coastal city of Dor to crush the revolt. At the head of the provincial force rode an ambitious young general named Seron. The army marched down the Mediterranean coast, then turned east to force open the main road to Jerusalem by way of Lydda and the steep ascent of Beth-horon. Seron's army was at least twice the size of Apollonius's.

Judah chose the steep and narrow pass between the villages of Lower Beth-horon and Upper Beth-horon as the place of battle. According to Jewish sources, the Maccabean army now numbered about 1,200 men, including Judah's specially trained band of Maccabean fighters called the Company of Faithful. Again, Judah divided his army into three groups: two on either side in concealed positions, and at the top of the pass, Judah himself, at the head of his Company of Faithful.

Seron made certain not to repeat the mistakes of Apollonius: His men, dressed in full armor, marched in battle positions. Up they climbed on the steep, narrow, winding road through the pass. Suddenly, Judah showed himself and his elite Company of Faithful to the enemy. Seeing the small rebel force holding the pass, Seron decided that his men, with their overwhelming numbers, could drive through the Maccabean position. Seron, with his forward phalanx, urged his men on to engage the rebels.

Judah watched as the long column of enemy troops toiled up the steep hill. When they were completely in his trap, Judah sounded the shofars. Archers and slingers fired down into the attacking Seleucid ranks. Then Judah and the Company of Faithful rushed down the steep road in a shock attack, tearing bloody gaps in the enemy battle line with their sickle swords, which in close quarters were more effective than the Seleucid provincials' 18-foot-long spears. The front lines of the enemy were routed. Seron, the Seleucid general, was killed.

Judah then signaled for a general attack and his men poured down the slopes of the pass. The enemy panicked, tore off their armor, threw down their weapons, and fled. The Maccabees chased the survivors as far as the coastal plains. More than 800 Seleucid soldiers died, a relatively small number considering the total rout they suffered, but the rebels were as interested in gathering the discarded arms as they were in slaughtering the defeated enemy.

"Thus began the fear of Judah and of his brethren," records 1 Maccabees, "and the dread fell upon the nations round about them. And his name came near even the king; and every nation told of the battles of Judah."

The imperial court in Antioch now realized that the empire was faced with a major rebellion. The deaths of two generals and the defeat of two armies could not be dismissed as the result of mere tactical lapses committed by provincial forces in the pursuit of a small band of Jewish fighters. Antioch had underestimated the power of the Maccabean forces.

> *His zeal and fearlessness, his military instinct and prudence, were alike evinced in this his first regular battle [at Beth-horon], and his choice of position, guarding the top of this dangerous pass, showed qualities beyond those of a mere bandit chief.*
> —CLAUDE REIGNIER CONDER
> on Judah Maccabee

But before Antiochus IV could deal with the Maccabean revolt, he first had to go to the eastern provinces. The imperial treasury was approaching bankruptcy because of constant warfare and the lavish public displays that Antiochus IV often sponsored, and soon he would have to make another huge tribute payment to the Romans. So, accompanied by half the imperial army, Antiochus IV went east to plunder places of worship as he had done in Jerusalem. And, as had happened in Judea, he met with considerable opposition in the eastern provinces of the empire. His problems there were compounded by the increasing strength of the Parthian Empire, which was pressing in on his eastern borders.

Before leaving, Antiochus IV left his viceroy, Lysias, in charge of the western half of the empire and directed him to crush the Jewish revolt. Lysias, with the other half of the imperial forces at his disposal, sent a large army to Palestine under the command of the generals Nicanor and Gorgias, men of wide experience.

It was this army — not merely a provincial detachment, but a royal army consisting in large part of imperial troops — that Judah defeated at the celebrated Battle of Emmaus in 165 B.C.

At this point it is important to note that the only sources available to give actual manpower figures for the armies involved in the revolt are Jewish sources, which in all cases depict the Maccabean forces as being greatly outnumbered. Bezalel Bar-Kochva, an Israeli historian writing in 1973, analyzed the military history of the Seleucid Empire in an effort to fill in the many gaps left in the record. He concluded that although the writers of 1 and 2 Maccabees apparently gave fairly accurate manpower figures for the small battles prior to Emmaus, they seem to have deliberately misrepresented the number of soldiers involved at Emmaus and in subsequent battles. For instance, 1 Maccabees gives the Seleucid troop strength at Emmaus as 47,000, but Bar-Kochva believes it could not have exceeded 20,000.

According to Bar-Kochva, "The traditional description of the Jewish few and weak who bravely withstood the royal force is based on the misleading picture presented by the Jewish sources, which for didactic purposes concealed the units and manpower at Judah Maccabee's disposal. But analysis of the sources suggests that the Jews were often superior in number and, though inferior in weapons, they were not unarmed but had phalanx and cavalry units."

Whatever the true size of the armies involved, Emmaus represented a surprising defeat for the Seleucids that left Lysias even more determined to mount a crushing blow against the Maccabean forces. During the next year he gathered another imperial army, collected intelligence, and laid his plans.

For a full year, Judah had time to organize his army, which according to Jewish sources now swelled to 10,000 men, though Bar-Kochva believes it was actually closer to 20,000. With trained and battle-hardened men, armed with captured weapons, Judah was now in complete control of Judea. Yet he was under no illusion about the limit to Maccabean military strength. Controlling the Judean countryside was one thing, but to retake Jerusalem and conquer the Acra would be a military effort of a totally different scope.

The Acra fortress was well built, its walls strong, its arsenal well stocked. Philip of Phrygia, the commander of the Acra, was a competent leader and protected the walls with seasoned soldiers. Judah knew that he lacked the strength or means to penetrate the fortified ramparts of the Acra. He had to remain content to train his soldiers, solidify his hold on the Judean countryside, and wait for the next Seleucid military onslaught.

After the defeat at Emmaus, Lysias himself was now forced to deal personally with the Maccabees. In the spring of 164 B.C., Lysias and his army, which according to Jewish sources numbered 60,000 infantry and 5,000 cavalry, moved south along the friendly coastal plains past Judea, then turned east through the province of Idumaea, whose inhabit-

A 5th-century B.C. figure of a Greek archer. Though the Seleucids had great advantages in numbers and weaponry during the early stages of the revolt, with the capture of equipment and an influx of trained Jewish soldiers who had served in the Seleucid and Egyptian armies the Maccabean forces soon drew even.

An illustration from a 10th-century manuscript of the Books of the Maccabees, showing the Seleucid cavalry in retreat. By 164 B.C., Judah had defeated four Seleucid armies and won a truce from Lysias, regent of the empire. In three years, the Maccabees and their allies had taken control of Judea.

ants supported the Seleucids against the Judeans. Lysias, a crafty general, showed he had learned from the previous defeats. At Marisa, the Seleucid army massed in battle formation and marched along the ridges of the mountain range rather than over the dangerous valley roads or mountain passes. The army arrived at the southern border fortress of Beth-zur and quickly took the lightly defended town. Judah and his forces were now in real danger. The enemy was within 16 miles — one day's march — of Jerusalem.

Judah, with his shorter lines of communication, could shadow the Seleucid army as it moved south and east. He kept his men safely within the steep, hilly terrain of Judea. Judah had few options open to him. He could not confront so large an army head-on, and Lysias was unlikely to divide his army as Nicanor had done at Emmaus. The only choice was to attack the army as it marched. This meant that the rebels would have to operate far from their base at Gophna, and therefore they would instead have to make their stand in the southern Judean hills, where the gentler grades were less obstructive to the Seleucids' phalanx battle lines.

While Lysias camped, Judah gathered all the men available to him. An army of 10,000, armed with captured Seleucid weapons, stood ready to block the road to Jerusalem. Judah divided his troops into small, mobile units of 1,000 men. The night before the Seleucids broke camp, Judah moved his units into position for battle. A mile north of Beth-zur, the road narrowed into a gully where Lysias would be unable to move the army forward in battle array. Judah positioned units on each side of the gully to harass the enemy and another unit to seal the narrow road.

By late morning a large vanguard of Seleucid soldiers had moved through and taken up position. In a daring, slashing attack, Judah directed his men to slice through the columns of soldiers leaving the narrow gully and separate the Seleucid vanguard from the main body of troops. Units of Maccabees on either side rained down arrows on the enemy in the valley. The Seleucid soldiers in the pass fled back to the main body of troops in confusion.

With the road secure, Judah directed his Company of Faithful to attack the isolated vanguard, which was soon crushed under the superior numbers of the Maccabee forces. Five thousand Seleucid soldiers died in the close fighting. Lysias, unable to stage a counterattack, realized he had underrated the skill, strength, and determination of Judah Maccabee and his fighters. He withdrew his army to Beth-zur.

On October 15, 164 B.C., Lysias, recognizing he could not defeat the Maccabean forces with the army he had, offered a compromise treaty to the Jews through the high priest Menelaus. Any rebels who laid down their weapons and returned home would be allowed to live in accordance with their own religious laws.

Judah withdrew, allowed the treaty to take effect, and waited until Lysias and his army returned to Antioch.

*It was Judas who first dared to withstand the foreign tyranny which threatened to annihilate the Jewish faith, and it was the genius of Judas which first pointed out the measures, military and political, by which independence might be best preserved.*
—CLAUDE REIGNIER CONDER
British historian

זה המטרה ואהרן חטת שמן במירות "

# 6

# The Temple Regained and the Sword of Israel

The October treaty made no mention of Judah or his rebel troops. It was written as an act of royal grace from the Seleucid viceroy Lysias to Menelaus, high priest and leader of Judea. Menelaus was still in control of Jerusalem and the Temple but only because of the protection of the Seleucid garrison in the Acra. But the withdrawal of Lysias and the Seleucid army signaled the impending defeat of Menelaus and his Jewish Hellenizers. To Judah and his followers, these victories seemed explicit confirmation from God of Judah Maccabee's authority and leadership in Judea. Without rank of birth or political office, Judah was the undisputed leader of Judea.

From the beginning, Judah acted as the lawful leader of his people. Like the kings and judges of old Israel, he organized his forces according to the

*His whole life was passed in struggles for freedom, and in fighting the battles of his country; but his personal ambition was never gratified by any dignity bestowed on him.*
—CLAUDE REIGNIER CONDER
on Judah Maccabee

A 13th-century illustration of the seven-branched candelabrum, a symbol of Judaism. In 164 B.C., Judah and his forces took control of the Temple, cleansed it, and rededicated it to Jewish worship. For many of the rebels, the central issue of the revolt — religious freedom — had been favorably resolved.

A view of the Temple site today, with the ruins of walls built by the Maccabees. Although the Temple was under Judean control, the Acra fortress just a few hundred feet away was still held by a hostile, well-armed Seleucid garrison, the high priest Menelaus, and the Jewish Hellenizers.

Law. That meant that any man who had built a house, was engaged to be married, planted a vineyard, or was fainthearted was excused from battle. His followers put aside their first fruits and tithes to be offered at the Temple, although it was still in the hands of Menelaus and the Seleucid garrison.

Judah and his forces kept themselves hidden in the Gophna hills so they would not be caught breaking the treaty. He was determined to wrest control of the Temple away from Menelaus, the Hellenizers, and the Seleucids. At the end of the autumn of 164 B.C., when the crops were gathered and the harvest stored, Judah and his army moved over the rubble of Jerusalem's walls — still in ruins four years after Apollonius had sacked the city — and entered Jerusalem.

The stones and broken mortar of the walls littered the deserted streets. Gaping dark holes in some of the houses showed where Seleucid soldiers had attacked and killed those who had tried to hold out against them. The city was nearly empty, with only a few people scratching out a meager existence. Behind the impregnable walls of the Acra, Menelaus and the Hellenist Jews lived under the protection of the imperial garrison.

Judah and his men went through the ruined city destroying every pagan shrine they found in the marketplaces and at street intersections. The Maccabees garrisoned themselves on the eastern hill of Jerusalem, beside the Temple Mount. Judah probed and tested the strength of the Acra but found its walls and high towers, along with the Seleucid garrison of 2,000, too strong.

The Acra was positioned less than 200 yards from the Temple, close enough so that arrows shot from the fortress could easily reach the Temple. Judah stationed archers behind tall wicker shields in the Temple courtyard to keep the Acra walls clear of Seleucid bowmen.

1 Maccabees describes what happened once the Temple was secure. Judah gathered a group of or-

Before, during, and after Maccabean times, non-Jews were restricted to the Temple's outer courtyard. This tablet, written in Greek and posted on the Temple grounds, warned non-Jews that entry into the inner courtyard was forbidden and punishable by death.

thodox priests and together they went to the building. When they saw the horrible state the Temple was in, "they rent their garments, and made great lamentation, and put ashes on their heads; and they fell on their faces to the ground; and they blew the solemn blasts upon the trumpets, and cried unto heaven." The gates were burned, the buildings were in ruin, and the altar was covered with the dried blood of sacrificed pigs. A lattice area stood in the center of the courtyard where prostitutes had entertained drunken soldiers. Weeds and shrubs had overgrown the entire area so that it looked like a thicket.

Judah and his Maccabee soldiers did the work while the priests supervised. They scrubbed the ruins clean, cut back the plants, and removed idols and stones used in pagan worship. For weeks they deliberated over what to do with the altar profaned by pagan sacrifices. Finally, they dismantled it and put the profaned stones away, to be hidden on the Temple Mount until such time in the future when a prophet would appear to decide what to do with the stones. Then they built a new altar of rough uncut stones on the model of the old one. The buildings were repaired; new gates were made and hung. New sacred temple vessels were put in place and a new candelabrum lit the holy place of the Temple.

Then, according to 1 Maccabees:

> They rose early on the morning of the 25th day of the ninth month, which is the month of Kislev, in the year 148 [fifteenth of December, 164 B.C.], and they brought a sacrifice according to the Law upon the new altar of burnt offerings which they had built. At the very time of year and on the very day on which the Gentiles had profaned the altar, it was dedicated to the sound of singing and harps and lyres and cymbals. The entire people prostrated themselves and bowed and gave thanks to Heaven who had brought them victory. They celebrated the dedication of the altar for eight days.

This was the crowning glory of Judah Maccabee's struggle against the Seleucid Empire. He decreed

A menorah, the candelabrum used during Hanukkah, the holiday founded by Judah. The traditional Hanukkah tale surrounding Judah's cleansing of the Temple — that one day's worth of oil miraculously lasted for eight days — originated long after Maccabean times.

that the dedication of the Temple should be observed each year as a joyous holiday. Its length was set at eight days, the same length as the harvest holiday of Sukkoth, which had not been celebrated that year because of the war.

The Feast of the Dedication — Hanukkah — was the first Jewish festival not instituted by scripture. The holiday has been celebrated ever since Judah's rededication of the Temple and is still celebrated by Jews today. In Jewish homes lights are kindled in a special Hanukkah candelabrum, called a menorah, which has nine places for candles or oil. Two are lit on the first evening and another each night until all nine are lit.

The Talmud, the body of commentaries that illuminate and interpret Jewish law, dramatizes the holiday with a parable written long after the Maccabean era. According to the parable, all the oil for lighting candles in the Temple had been desecrated, with only enough unsullied oil to last for one day, which miraculously turned out to be enough for eight days. On Hanukkah, that and other stories are told, songs are sung, and prayers recited that recall the victories of Judah Maccabee. Hanukkah is the reminder to Jews and symbol to the world that the Jewish people will fight to preserve their traditions and worship of God.

After the rededication of the Temple, Judah and his followers proclaimed themselves the true Israel and he himself was accepted as both the temporal and spiritual leader of Judea. His army swelled to 22,000 men, including cavalry and infantrymen trained in the Seleucid style of massed, phalanx warfare. Most of the best-trained soldiers were probably Jews from Egypt and Phrygia, as well as from neighboring countries in Palestine, who had served in imperial and provincial military units of the Egyptian and Seleucid empires. Judah's military forces were now numerically comparable to any army the Seleucids could muster against them.

To solidify his position against the Seleucid garrison in the Acra, Judah ordered the building of high walls and strong towers around the Temple. He quartered Maccabee troops in the fortifications to protect it against raids from the Acra. The Beth-zur fortress, 16 miles south of Jerusalem, was fortified to defend the capital against a return of the imperial armies. Judah was the master of Judea. Only the Acra remained as a refuge for those loyal to the Seleucid Empire.

Firmly in control of Judea, Judah next turned to matters in the rest of Palestine, beyond the borders of his home province. He was able to do so because the Seleucid Empire was in turmoil. Antiochus IV Epiphanes — whose violent and erratic behavior in both his public and private life had by now earned him the mocking nickname "Epimanes" (madman) — was far away from Palestine, fighting in the east-

*Wherefore if thou dost not prevent them quickly, they will do greater things than these, neither shalt thou be able to rule them.*

—MEMBERS OF THE
SELEUCID KINGDOM
asking Antiochus IV to act
against the increasingly
rebellious Jews

ern provinces of Persia. Though Antiochus IV was at least temporarily successful in his eastern battles, he nevertheless failed to collect enough money to pay his army. Meanwhile, Lysias, the viceroy, had retreated to Antioch in the face of Maccabean opposition. This left Judah free to cope with developments in the rest of Palestine.

Most of Judea's neighbors in Palestine were hostile toward the Maccabees. When Antiochus IV's decrees abolishing the Jewish religion were put into effect, some of the neighboring provinces had taken the opportunity to settle age-old scores against the Judeans by attacking, enslaving, or massacring their local Jewish populations. Uncertain as to how to deal with subsequent Judean successes and without leadership from Antioch, the provincial governors made their own policies in an effort to discourage further Judean advances.

The newly appointed governor of Idumaea, Gorgias, one of the defeated generals at the Battle of

An aerial view of the Israeli seaport of Jaffa, a Phoenician city during Maccabean times. After Judah crushed the Seleucids' provincial armies, the predominantly non-Jewish population of Jaffa retaliated by massacring the Jews of the city.

Emmaus, hired mercenaries to attack the Jews and encouraged the cities in his province to oppress their Jewish populations. Elsewhere, the people of the Phoenician city of Jaffa took the city's Jews and drowned them in the sea. The persecution of local Jews was a gesture of defiance toward Judah and his forces made at a safe distance. This persecution was profitable for the local citizens: They could seize the possessions of their victims and enhance their political status with Antioch. More important, it might save their region from being identified with the rebel cause — and thus from devastation by imperial forces.

Fugitive Jews straggled into Judea and begged for help from Judah. He gathered an army to move out beyond the Judean borders and rescue their fellow Jews. Once again, Seleucid government officials underestimated the Jewish general. They had not expected him to operate outside his own hilly province, and if he did, they were certain they could defeat him once he was away from familiar territory.

Word came that Jews were under attack in the province of Idumaea, just south of Judea. With a small, carefully picked army of 3,000, Judah moved out. In a quick, punishing raid he crushed the Idumaeans and took a large amount of loot.

The Judean troops, not weighted down with heavy weapons or supplies, turned east and quickly marched against the Beonite tribe, who had closed the roads between Judea and the Nabataean nation. The Nabataeans, a tribal people who had moved northward from Arabia into the Negev desert and what is today called Jordan, managed to retain their independence despite all Seleucid efforts to conquer them. These enemies of the Seleucids gladly assisted Judah Maccabee in his fight against Judea's hostile neighbors. In a series of raids, Judah killed the leader of the Beonites, slaughtered many more of the tribesmen, set fire to their fortress, and tore down the towers they had built alongside the roads.

Judah returned to Jerusalem to hear that the plight of other Jews was even worse. In Arbata, a city on the coastal plains, Jews were being besieged

The massacre of Jewish townspeople in Jaffa was repeated in cities throughout the surrounding, mainly non-Jewish provinces in Palestine. In reprisal, Judah's forces ranged through the region in 164 B.C., laying waste to several cities.

by an army from the Phoenician cities of Ptolemaïs, Tyre, and Sidon. Also, the cities of the northeastern hill province of Gilead had imprisoned their Jews. In Gilead, some Jews had fled to the fortress of Diathema and were under siege there. The situation was desperate. Judah took immediate action. He divided his army: Simon, Judah's older brother, took 3,000 soldiers and headed north for Arbata; Judah, with his brother Jonathan and 8,000 soldiers, headed northeast for Gilead. These campaigns were not undertaken to conquer territory but to punish the hostile Gentiles and evacuate the Jews.

Simon had the smaller force because he had a shorter distance to cover and the enemy army lacked the military support of a Seleucid governor. Simon won a series of battles in and around Arbata and chased the Seleucid provincial forces to the gates of Ptolemaïs. On his way back to Jerusalem, he gathered the besieged Jews and took them to Judea. They returned to Jerusalem with great rejoicing.

Judah's campaign was much more complex. When he had listened to all the possible intelligence on the strength, defenses, and location of the Seleucid general Timotheus and his army, he decided to move east across the desert with the Maccabean forces instead of taking the easier route north. The Maccabees marched east to the Jordan River, crossed it, and made a three-day march northeast. They were led through the desert by Nabataean guides and given supplies.

This three-day march put Judah on the eastern side of the Gilead province, a completely unexpected direction for the Maccabees' attack. Bozrah was the first city to fall to the Maccabean forces. After it fell, Judah changed direction and marched northwest to the walled fortress of Diathema, where the local Jews were trying to defend themselves.

In a night march over the open desert, Judah and his army moved the remarkable distance of 31 miles right up to the walls of Diathema. It was dawn when they approached the fortress, and Judah had organized his force into three units while on the move. The army of Timotheus was ready with scaling ladders and siege engines to take the fortress of Diathema. Judah surprised and trapped them against the walls of the fortress while the defending Jews rained arrows down on the Seleucid soldiers. The Maccabees inflicted heavy casualties on them in the hand-to-hand fighting that followed. The army of Timotheus was routed.

Judah knew his time was limited and that he was far from home, supplies, and reinforcements. He divided his forces in the face of the enemy. In a rapid succession of marches, he attacked and took the cities of Casphor, Maked, and Bezer. The Maccabees dealt ruthlessly with the people of Bezer for massacring the local Jews by burning the city and slaughtering all its male inhabitants.

A threatening Seleucid army moved down from the north. The defeated general Timotheus had escaped to Damascus and raised a new army, which the Jewish sources number at 20,000. Through his spies, Judah was kept informed of this army's movement. Timotheus and his army camped at the stream beside the city of Raphon. The stream was a torrent filled by late spring rains and Timotheus believed Judah would not cross in the face of his larger army.

Judah posted his officers at the edge of the water and instructed them to advance into battle. Leading his men across the stream, Judah attacked the army and smashed it. The tribe of Arab warriors that fought beside Timotheus sued for peace by giving Judah a gift of cattle. The remnants of the defeated Seleucid army, meanwhile, fled to the city of Carnaim. Judah and his forces followed and took the city. The Seleucid soldiers hid in the temple of Atargatis, but Judah burned it down with the soldiers inside.

A caravan of refugee Jews whom Judah had liberated from the defeated cities of Gilead formed for the long march to Judea. The army of the Maccabees shielded them from any attacks. On the road to Judea the city of Ephron barricaded the road and refused them passage. In a battle lasting a day and a night the Maccabees stormed the city with captured siege equipment, took the city, killed all the men, and burned it. In the city of Scythopolis, the Maccabees, who by this time had devastated most of Gilead, were given entry and a place to rest without opposition. The caravan finally reached Jerusalem and was greeted with joy and thanksgiving.

Not all the news in Jerusalem was good. Judah had left two commanders in charge of the home army while he was away with orders not to engage the enemy. They disobeyed the command, engaged the forces of Gorgias, and were defeated with a loss of 2,000 men.

Judah restored Maccabee dominance in a series of raids against the Phoenician city of Jaffa and avenged the Jewish civilians drowned there by burning all the ships in port; in Jamnia he also razed the port. In a southern campaign against Idumaea, Judah burned the city of Hebron. Near Mar-

> *But now I remember the evils that I did at Jerusalem, and that I took all the vessels of gold and silver that were therein, and sent to destroy the inhabitants of Judea without cause. I perceive, therefore that for this cause these troubles are come upon me, and behold, I perish through great grief in a strange land.*
> —ANTIOCHUS IV
> according to 2 Maccabees, regretting his cruelty toward the Jews, just before his death

isa, Judah defeated Gorgias once again and almost captured him. The Maccabees then turned west and took the Philistine city of Azotus, looted it, and destroyed its pagan temples.

These battles secured the borders of Judea and coerced the rest of Palestine into stopping the oppression of Jews. The Maccabees were now an army to be reckoned with, able to save not only themselves, but Jews beyond their frontiers. In Judea once again, Jews lived in freedom. Still the Acra held out as the bastion of Seleucid control.

In Antioch, events had taken place that would change the course of the Judean future. In 163 B.C., Antiochus IV, fighting in Persia with his army, decided to plunder a temple in the city of Elymaïs. With a token force he tried to seize the temple but was driven off by the inhabitants and only narrowly

**With Judea firmly in Maccabean hands, Judah's forces moved beyond the province's borders, rescuing besieged Jews in cities throughout the rest of Palestine. In one of his victories, at a stream near the village of Raphon, Judah defeated a Seleucid army led by the general Timotheus.**

escaped with his life. Antiochus, a broken man ruling a disintegrating empire, died soon after.

The king's death left his empire in confusion. As he neared death, he relinquished control to Philip, the general of his crack troops, the Companions. Philip was to replace the defeated viceroy, Lysias, and rule the kingdom until Antiochus IV's 11-year-old son, Antiochus V Eupator ("Well-fathered"), came of age. The collision between the rival generals for the power of the regency was now locked on course. Civil war could be the only outcome.

Things had never looked better for the Maccabees in Judea.

# 7

# The Empire Attacks

The Seleucid garrison in the Acra, though too small in number to stop Judah, continued to harass Temple worshipers. Archers fired arrows into the Temple courtyard and killed Jews at prayer. Once soldiers sallied out from the Acra and killed a group of priests as they arrived at the Temple for the morning sacrifice.

Judah decided to use captured siege equipment to end the problem of the Acra once and for all. The Maccabees built battering rams and erected earthwork walls around the Acra. After many weeks they found the citadel's ramparts too high and strong for them to take — the walls were too thick for battering rams and the breaching equipment they had captured proved too crude. None of the Maccabees had enough siege experience to weaken the Acra walls by tunneling beneath their foundations. Judah was forced to wait out the siege and try to starve the defenders into surrender. But the Seleucids had cut tunnels from the interior of the Acra to hidden escape routes beyond its walls and used them to send messengers past the Maccabee forces.

*And he [Judah] went about the cities of Judea, and destroyed the ungodly out of the land, and turned away wrath from Israel.*
—I MACCABEES

**Eleazar became the first of the Maccabee brothers to die. In an effort to rally the Judean troops at the Battle of Beth-zechariah, he tried to kill a Seleucid war elephant; the wounded animal fell and crushed him. The Maccabees suffered their first major defeat at the battle and were forced to fall back to Jerusalem.**

A medieval manuscript showing the Seleucid cavalry fighting Judah's cavalry. With Antiochus IV dead, Lysias tried to seize power. To gain the imperial army's support he again moved on Judea, assembling a force of 55,000 to end the Maccabean revolt once and for all.

Messengers from the beleaguered Acra arrived in Antioch with pleas for Lysias to come to their aid. As Lysias listened, he was torn between the struggle over the regency with Philip and the revolt in Judea. But his defeat at the hands of the Maccabee rebels was a stain on his honor; a victory over the Maccabees would restore the imperial army's confidence in him, bring Judea's neighbors into line, and show the Roman and Egyptian empires that a new strongman was in control of Antioch. His choice was clear: He would destroy the Maccabees.

Lysias gathered all the forces available to him and, in the name of the 11-year-old king, Antiochus V Eupator, marched on Judea. According to 1 Maccabees, the army consisted of 100,000 infantry, 20,000 cavalry, and 32 war elephants, but later sources say the Seleucid army numbered 50,000 infantry, 5,000 cavalry, and 8 elephants. Modern researchers agree with the latter set of figures. Whatever the true numbers, the Seleucids' use of elephants was an unusual gesture of defiance against Rome, because the Magnesia treaty banned the Seleucids from using elephants in battle. That Lysias would violate the treaty with Rome demonstrates how important he felt his battle with the Maccabees was. Lysias was counting on the terror these huge animals would induce among the Judean forces, many of whom would be seeing them for the first time.

The Seleucid army was a traveling carnival complete with merchants and wizards. Lysias even brought along his racehorses and high-ranking nonmilitary officials. This formidable army of 55,000 troops moved south against Judea in the late spring of 163 B.C.

The problem for Lysias was how to draw Judah into battle without opening himself up to ambush. As Lysias marched along the coastal plains past Judea, Judah shadowed the Seleucid army. Near the town of Modin, where the revolt had begun, Judah made a daring night raid on the Seleucid encampment.

A stone figure of a Greek boy of noble lineage. Antiochus IV's 11-year-old son, Antiochus V Eupator, was crowned king, but Lysias held real power. Antiochus V may have been on hand when Lysias's army closed in on Jerusalem.

A catapult used in ancient siege warfare. While Lysias approached Jerusalem, Judah laid siege to the Acra fortress alongside the Temple. He was forced to lift the siege when Lysias arrived and in turn attacked the Maccabean forces in the Temple compound.

With a small, handpicked detachment, he moved out under the cover of night from the protection of the steep Judean hills. He gave his men the password "God's Victory." They crawled past the guards and attacked the men around the king's quarters, killing 2,000 Seleucid soldiers in the dark. They set fire to tents, spreading terror and confusion in the Seleucid army. As the Maccabee raiders made their escape, they killed an elephant and its trainer.

Again, Lysias had underestimated the daring of the Jewish general. He moved his army farther west, away from the Judean borders, so that Judah could not surprise him again. At Beth-zur, Lysias turned north but found his way blocked by the Jewish garrison at Beth-zur's fortress.

Lysias attacked the fortress. Although its fortifications were not particularly strong, the besieged defenders fought courageously. The army of Lysias was brought to a halt when they could not take the fortress by storm. Siege engines were erected, and Lysias began the methodical process of battering down the walls of Beth-zur. In a daring strike, the defenders sallied out and burned the siege engines.

Judah tried to supply the Maccabee defenders of the fort but failed. Jewish sources blame the defeat on the treachery of a Jewish soldier named Rodokos, who is said to have told Lysias of a secret passageway to the fortress of Beth-zur. Rodokos was caught and killed by the Maccabee defenders.

Without supplies the position of the defenders quickly grew more serious. Lysias built new siege engines and attacked with renewed vigor. Judah was forced to lift his own siege of the Acra and try to relieve the defenders of Beth-zur.

Supplies were short throughout Judea because it was a Jewish sabbatical year. The Law commanded that every seven years the fields lie fallow and crops not be harvested. As a result, provisions for both armies were low.

As Judah hurried south from Jerusalem, his position was perilous. The Seleucid army was so large he could not repeat his tactical guerrilla pattern of battle. Judah must have hoped that surprise, the Maccabees' courage, and his leadership would overcome the odds. If he melted away into the hills, he stood to lose all that he had gained during the past three years of fighting.

Lysias was not about to be surprised again by the Maccabee forces. Five miles north of Beth-zur, near a town called Beth-zechariah situated on a large plateau, Lysias positioned his troops to engage the Maccabees. At daybreak, Lysias deployed his army and attacked the Maccabees.

For the first time, Judah was forced to fight from a defensive position. To the waiting Maccabean forces, the sight of this enormous army must have been a terrifying sight. The Seleucids advanced in a broad battle line, in the center of which were the armored elephants, each surrounded by a densely packed phalanx unit of 1,000 infantry and 500 specially trained heavy cavalry. (Unless specially trained, horses will bolt at the sight of elephants.) Spearmen and archers rode on the backs of the elephants in special wooden turrets. The charging elephants, which before the battle had been goaded into a frenzy by being exposed to the smell of alcohol, were used to tear a gap in the Maccabee line so the

> *Let us be friends with these men, and make peace with them, and with all their nation; and convenant with them, that they shall live after their laws, as they did before.*
> —LYSIAS
> suggesting to Antiochus IV that the Seleucids make peace with the Jews

Beth-zechariah, site of the battle where Eleazar died, as it appears today. The victory here enabled Lysias to besiege the Temple. Judah and the last remnants of the rebel army, short on food and supplies, were near surrender when Lysias lifted the siege and returned to Antioch to battle for the Seleucid throne.

accompanying infantry could pour into the rifts. The rest of the cavalry was posted on the wings of the battle line to protect them from flanking attacks by the Maccabees, and light infantry stood by to fill in any gaps that might open in the Seleucid line of battle. The battle line, almost a mile in length, was deployed over the whole plateau, from the heights to the low ground.

The Seleucids moved forward in step to the sound of horns and drums. The marching soldiers shouted a cadence as they marched and slapped their shields against their bronze breastplates. The ground shook with the noise so that the Maccabee soldiers could not hear the shouts of their own commanders.

Against the 55,000 Seleucids, the Judeans had 20,000 soldiers. Judah struck with all the religious zeal he could inspire in his troops. They angled away from the elephants and tried to flank the phalanx center but were thrown back. The Seleucid army moved ponderously forward behind the elephants, undeterred by the Maccabee charge.

In desperate times, desperate measures are needed. Eleazar, the youngest of the five sons of Mattathias, led a suicidal charge with a detachment of men against the largest elephant. He naively supposed that because the elephant wore the breastplate and banner of the king, the king would be riding on it. Driving through the Seleucid ranks, Eleazar reached the elephant. Boldly, he rushed beneath the elephant and ripped its stomach open with a sword thrust. The enraged animal crushed him to death. To this day, an ancient oak marks the place where, in the words of 1 Maccabees, Eleazar "gave himself to deliver his people and to acquire an everlasting name."

Eleazar's sacrifice was futile, and the Maccabee forces were completely routed. Judah, trying to hold together what remained of his army, retreated to Jerusalem, six miles to the north. The Maccabees were determined to make a final stand behind the walls around the Temple. Lysias, meanwhile, returned to Beth-zur and completed the siege. The defenders of Beth-zur, knowing now that no rescue could occur, took the generous terms offered by Lysias and surrendered. The disaster at Beth-zechariah suddenly put the entire Maccabean cause within one battle of total defeat.

The full force of the royal Seleucid army now gathered in Jerusalem around the walls of Mount Zion, where the Temple stood. After five years of entrapment, the defenders of the Acra were liberated. The Seleucid army stormed the walls of the Temple Mount but were repulsed, so they turned to the long process of battering down the fortifications.

Lysias built a siege wall around Mount Zion's walls. Siege engines were built, as were catapults for throwing stones and incendiary missiles, ballistae for launching darts, battering rams, and wooden

An ancient Greek depiction of an assassination. With another Seleucid-Maccabean truce in effect, Lysias ordered the walls of the Temple complex torn down while agreeing to execute the Hellenist high priest Menelaus. But upon their return to Antioch, Lysias and Antiochus V were assassinated by Demetrius, a contender for the throne.

towers so Seleucid archers could shoot arrows onto the defending walls. Judah countered with his own catapults and ballistae, but soon it became apparent that hunger was the main enemy of the Maccabees. The defenders had run out of food. Judah released most of his troops to disperse into the countryside; only a select few stayed behind with him.

But unexpectedly, the Seleucids lifted the siege. They too were suffering from hunger; furthermore, Lysias had gotten word that Philip was with his army at the gates of Antioch, ready to install himself as ruler of the empire. When Philip occupied Antioch, Lysias had no choice but to hurry home.

Lysias offered generous terms for peace that Judah could not refuse. All decrees of Antiochus IV Epiphanes were abolished. The Jews were granted total freedom of worship, and Lysias promised to protect the Jews in the exercise of their laws and religion. Amnesty was given to Judah and the rebels. In return, the Judeans agreed to end the revolt and recognize Antiochus V as king and Lysias as regent.

After the treaty was accepted, Lysias was allowed to enter the Temple complex. He saw how strong the walls were and ordered them torn down. The Maccabees were helpless to stop him.

Lysias returned to Antioch, taking the high priest Menelaus with him. In Berea, on the way to Antioch, Lysias stopped to execute Menelaus by roasting him over a fire. It was an especially horrible death reserved in ancient times for temple robbers. Upon arriving at Antioch, Lysias took the city by storm, killed Philip, and ruled as regent with the young king.

Now that Menelaus was dead and the goal of religious freedom had been obtained, the Hasidim, the backbone of the Maccabean army, left Judah and returned to their homes. Judah retired to his base in the Gophna hills, accompanied by the remnants of the rebel army. There he waited for a reversal in Seleucid policy.

# 8

# The War for Independence Resumes

The war for religious freedom had ended. The Hasidim were content as long as they were allowed to follow the Torah and worship God in the Temple unmolested. But for Judah this was not enough. He believed that only when Judea had political freedom could Jews be certain of their religious freedom. Before Antiochus IV's anti-Jewish decrees it had never occurred to Jews that anyone would ever seek to destroy them because of their religion. But it had happened and it might happen again, especially in light of the changeability of Seleucid policy. The bloody palace intrigues and open warfare between rivals for the throne, virtually an annual feature of Seleucid politics, could at any moment leave the Judeans facing a new king — one who might not honor the treaty Lysias had signed with Judah.

But even with the treaty in effect, Judah had reason to doubt the authenticity of Lysias's pledge to honor Jewish religious freedom. Lysias appointed

*What had begun as a religious revolt soon developed, however, into a strong nationalistic movement for political independence.*
—D. S. RUSSELL
on the aspirations
of the Jews

**The Triumph of Judas Macchabée, painted in 1635 by the Flemish master Peter Paul Rubens, depicts Judah's victory in 161 B.C. over the army led by the Seleucid general Nicanor, whose head was brought back to Jerusalem as a trophy. It was Judah's last great victory.**

In 162 B.C., **Demetrius I became emperor by overthrowing and executing Antiochus V and Lysias. He continued the war against the Maccabees, appointing as high priest the Hellenizer Alcimus and assigning Nicanor to lead the Seleucid forces in Judea.**

a new high priest, Alcimus, another Jew who belonged to the party of Hellenizers. It is unclear exactly when Alcimus actually began his duties, but 2 Maccabees suggests that the Maccabean party forcibly prevented him from assuming office for at least a year.

Meanwhile, in 162 B.C., another power struggle broke out in Antioch. A nephew of Antiochus IV's, Demetrius, escaped or was allowed to escape from Rome, where he had lived as a hostage under the terms of the Magnesia treaty. In short order, Demetrius made his way to Syria, staged a coup d'état, captured his young cousin Antiochus V and the regent Lysias, and executed them. Now the Seleucid king was Demetrius I Soter ("Redeemer"). One of his first acts was to confirm Alcimus, who had fled to Antioch as a result of Maccabean pressure, as the rightful high priest of Judea.

Demetrius I moved quickly to reinstall Alcimus at the Temple in Jerusalem, assigning the task to Bacchides, the new governor-general of all the provinces in the western half of the empire. Bacchides marched into Jerusalem and reinstated Alcimus as high priest, winning the trust of the Hasidim by assuring them that Alcimus's rule would be just. Before Bacchides returned to Antioch, he made a show of strength. Not far from Jerusalem, in the town of Ber-zetha, Bacchides rounded up the Maccabean collaborators and executed them. Judah's forces were so reduced that he could not challenge the Seleucid general.

Alcimus, now certain of imperial support and seeing that the Maccabees were unable to respond, reneged on Bacchides's pledge. He rounded up 60 leaders of the Hasidim and executed them. The Hasidic party, outraged, joined forces with the Maccabees once again. Judah's army was rejuvenated, and new fighting broke out between the Maccabeans and the Hellenizers. Judah again marched into Jerusalem and took possession of the Temple. Alcimus once again fled to Antioch.

Demetrius I, determined to assert his authority against the rebellious Maccabees and Hasidim, decided to send an army to Jerusalem to install Alcimus by force. He appointed a general, Nicanor (not the same Nicanor who was defeated at Emmaus), to lead the army. Nicanor arrived in Jerusalem with offers of peace.

According to 2 Maccabees, Nicanor and Judah became friends. Nicanor urged Judah to marry, which he did. Judah lived in peace and "partook of life's blessings." Alcimus, in Antioch, heard of the friendship between Judah and Nicanor and, according to the story, told Demetrius I. The king was enraged at Nicanor and sent a message ordering him to capture Judah and bring him to Antioch for trial. Nicanor was troubled but could not oppose the king and looked for a chance to capture Judah. Judah noticed Nicanor was rude when they next met, decided something was wrong, and fled to assemble his men.

Nicanor, according to the story in 2 Maccabees, realized he had been outsmarted and in anger went to the Temple. There he found priests offering sacrifices to God. Nicanor demanded that Judah be turned over to him, but the priests claimed they did not know where Judah was. Then Nicanor stretched his right hand forward and swore, "If you do not hand Judah over to me, I shall raze to the ground this shrine of your God and tear down the altar, and I shall build in its place a fine temple to Dionysus."

Both 1 and 2 Maccabees agree that Judah, having escaped Nicanor's attempt to capture him, gathered his army and closed the roads around Jerusalem, isolating Nicanor in the city. Nicanor responded by trying to force open the road that led northwest through Beth-horon to the friendly cities outside of Judea. In an indecisive battle at the small village of Caphor Salama, a few miles north of Jerusalem, Nicanor was turned back, leaving 500 dead on the battlefield.

The Jewish sources put the number of Maccabean troops at this point at 3,000. Though modern historians estimate that there were actually far more Maccabean troops, they nevertheless believe that the Judean forces were indeed significantly reduced from the mighty army of 22,000 that had existed just a little more than a year before. But they were

> *For as long as Judas liveth, it is not possible that the state should be quiet.*
> —DEMETRIUS I
> Seleucid emperor

**Although 1 and 2 Maccabees say that the Seleucids, as reflected in this Doré illustration, outnumbered the Judeans at the Battle of Adasa in 161 B.C., modern historians believe the two sides were evenly matched in number. However, the Seleucids broke their treaty with Rome by using war elephants — ancient warfare's equivalent of the tank.**

fired with religious zeal and Judah once again had an army dedicated to fighting the Seleucids.

Nicanor planned a combined operation with other Seleucid forces marching up from the coast to join him. Early in March 161 B.C., he slipped out from Jerusalem and joined up with the others at Beth-horon, halfway between Jerusalem and Modin. Nicanor's army at that point numbered about 10,000 men, most of whom were provincial troops.

They headed south, toward Jerusalem. At first they must have marched warily in battle formation, prepared for an ambush from Judah. As they marched and Judah did not attack them, Nicanor and his soldiers probably gained confidence, perhaps relaxing once they were within two hours of the city. Judah, meanwhile, kept track of every movement the Seleucid army made through reports from his observers. On the plains near the village of Adasa, about four miles north of Jerusalem, he sprang his trap on the Seleucid army. Nicanor himself was one of the first to die.

Nicanor's death decided the fate of the battle. The Seleucid troops panicked, and, because the Maccabees were attacking from the south, they were unable to flee toward Jerusalem. The defeated army had to make the difficult passage over the mountains toward the royal fortress of Gazara, 15 miles away. The road took the fleeing army along the Chephirah ridge, past villages friendly to the Maccabees. Judah had the trumpets sounded to alert the villages. A complete rout followed with the villagers joining the attacking Maccabee forces. The Seleucid soldiers, retreating in utter confusion, were found and slaughtered throughout the day and into the night. Nicanor's army was destroyed.

Judah found Nicanor's body and ordered that the head and right arm up to the shoulder be cut off and taken to Jerusalem. He had the head and arm nailed to a wall opposite the Temple for all to see God's retribution for Nicanor's threat to raze the holy sanctuary. The victory had come during the Jewish festival of Purim, which celebrated the failure of a plot to annihilate the Jews living in Babylon in about 550 B.C. Now there was an additional cause for celebration. Judah declared the day of Nicanor's defeat to be a holiday known as the "Day of Nicanor." It was celebrated annually for hundreds of years, though eventually it was abandoned.

Judah Maccabee had beaten back yet another attempt to destroy the Jewish religion. But the Seleucids would return once more.

Judah victorious after killing Nicanor and destroying his army at the Battle of Adasa, as depicted by the 17th-century Dutch painter Gerard Van Honthorst. The victory was celebrated as "Nicanor's Day," a holiday for hundreds of years. But unlike Hanukkah, the other festival proclaimed by Judah, the celebration of Nicanor's Day was eventually forgotten.

# 9

# The Lion of Judea Is Killed

Judah knew that the next advancing Seleucid army was only months away; all his victories could be overturned by one defeat. For help, he looked to the Romans, who, ever since the Battle of Magnesia in 190 B.C., held the upper hand against the Seleucids. The Roman republic was the strongest military power in the entire western half of the known world. The Romans were still a hundred years away from turning the Mediterranean Sea into their own private lake, but they were well on their way.

Judah sent two trusted men to Rome to plead the Jewish cause. Eupolemus, from the priestly family of Hakioz, and Jason made the long journey to appear before the 300 members of the Roman Senate. Their Greek names suggest these men came from upper-class families influenced by Hellenization; however, that they were chosen by Judah shows that they remained faithful to traditional Judaism. These educated men were well suited to argue the Maccabean cause before the Romans, who had long before adopted Hellenistic culture.

*But perhaps the most important act in Judas' career was the conclusion of a treaty with Rome. His foresight provided a protection for Jewish freedom and faith which probably saved them from utter extinction.*
—CLAUDE REIGNIER CONDER
British historian

**After Judah's death, his brothers Jonathan, Simon, and John carried on the war for Jewish independence. This 14th-century illustration depicts the battle in which Jonathan defeated the Seleucids in 157 B.C.**

Rome was favorably impressed by the Maccabees' ability to defeat Seleucid armies. The two Jewish ambassadors were quickly ushered before the Senate, and soon a treaty of friendly alliance between Rome and Judea was signed. The treaty was inscribed on tablets of bronze; one stayed in Rome and the other was sent to Judea. Like most treaties of alliance, this one was inspired by mutual need. The Judeans needed the threat of Roman intervention to make the Seleucids think twice before attacking again. The Romans hoped the threat of their intervention would force the Seleucids to gather still larger armies in their effort to overcome the rebellious Judeans, a move that would further drain Seleucid resources and thus strengthen Roman efforts at eastward expansion.

It is not recorded whether Judah expected any Roman military support; if he did, he was quickly disappointed. But the one thing Judah knew he would accomplish was gaining legitimacy for his sovereignty in Judea. The very existence of the

A frieze depicting the Roman Senate. The Senate approved a pact between Rome and Judea in 162 B.C., ensuring Roman intervention in the event of further Seleucid aggression against Judea. Though the Romans did nothing about the subsequent Seleucid invasion, Judea was nevertheless recognized as an independent nation with Judah as its ruler.

treaty meant that Rome was treating Judea as an independent Jewish state with Judah as its leader.

Because the courier service from Rome to Antioch was faster than to Judea, Demetrius I probably learned of the treaty before Judah. Demetrius I decided on immediate military action against the Maccabees. He had to show Rome he was the master of his empire's internal affairs, and he had to do so at once.

Bacchides, the governor-general, left Antioch at the head of the Right Wing, special crack troops of the Seleucid imperial army. This force linked up with about 10,000 provincial troops to make up an army of 20,000 infantry and 2,000 cavalry. Bacchides and his army marched south through the Jordan valley, deliberately taking the most difficult and least guarded route, through country where very few Jews lived. They reached a plateau about 15 miles north of Jerusalem and stopped to capture and kill Maccabean supporters in Arbela, close to the Gophna hills. As the historian Bezalel Bar-Kochva writes:

> After reaching the plateau Bacchides had a virtually clear road to Jerusalem, but he does not seem to have been in any hurry and tried, first of all, to establish control of the various routes in the region and terrorize the rural population. . . . Bacchides' main aim in the expedition was not the occupation of territories or mere military victory, but the liquidation of Judas Maccabaeus and his close adherents.

Judah could do little to stop Bacchides. Although the Jewish sources say that the manpower of the Maccabean forces had dwindled to 3,000 (and to 800 once the ensuing battle began), modern historians believe there were far more Judean soldiers at Judah's disposal, perhaps as many as the 20,000 Bacchides had. The real reason, they believe, that Judah was unable to ambush or otherwise dislodge Bacchides was that Judah had finally been outmaneuvered.

Bacchides established a base at Berea, eight miles north of Jerusalem, to cut Judah off from his rebel base in Gophna. Now the Seleucid general's heavily

*Wherefore hast thou [Demetrius] made thy yoke heavy upon our friends and confederates the Jews? If therefore they complain any more against thee, we will do them justice, and fight with thee by sea and by land.*
—THE ROMAN SENATE announcing its alliance with the Jews

equipped troops had control of all the roads leading into a relatively flat area, thus precluding any chance of a Maccabean ambush. Judah camped at the village of Ber-zetha and when Bacchides moved farther north, Judah moved in behind him to threaten him from the rear. At a place called Elasa, a mile west of Bacchides' camp at Berea, the two armies met in battle. The following account of the Battle of Elasa, which took place in April 160 B.C., is based on the reconstruction of the event offered by Bar-Kochva.

The attack was launched by the Seleucids. Bacchides organized his army, without the usual phalanx center, into two smaller, more maneuverable phalanx arms. The cavalry protected either flank. He repeated the tactic used to defeat the Maccabees at Beth-zechariah; the Right Wing under his command engaged Judah in a frontal attack while the other unit tried to outflank the Maccabee front. Bacchides also kept his cavalry out of the battle at first, so that it would be available to capture Judah if he tried to escape to Jerusalem.

The Judean phalanx held off the Seleucid phalanx, but could do no more than that. Judah had to do something to try and break the Seleucids. He chose to attack the Right Wing, perhaps in the hope of killing Bacchides and demoralizing the Seleucids as the death of Nicanor had done at Adasa the year before. Judah divided his forces in two and with the larger group charged the Right Wing, which fell back in retreat. Judah's cavalry led the chase and the infantry followed, drawing Judah farther away from the fighting between the phalanxes. Bacchides retreated to the mountain slope but kept order in the ranks of the Right Wing. Meanwhile the other Seleucid unit had driven the weaker Maccabee group from the field. This unit displayed discipline and did not chase the fleeing, defeated Maccabees; instead, it turned and fell on the rear of Judah's forces.

Judah was now confronted with enemy forces on both sides. According to 1 Maccabees, when Judah was urged to flee he said, "Heaven forbid that I should do such a thing as run away! If our time is

come, let us die bravely for our brothers and leave no stain on our honor!"

While Judah was occupied in fending off the attack from the rear, Bacchides was able to regroup and turn on the Maccabees from the front. The fighting had been fierce and had lasted for hours, and none of Judah's men were able to rest or even drink water during the battle. They fell, exhausted, unable to defend themselves from the Seleucids' assault on both front and rear. Judah, now surrounded, refused to surrender, purchasing every moment he could for his brothers Jonathan and Simon, who had retreated from the field with the smaller Judean contingent. "In the course of the fierce battle many fell slain on both sides," writes the author of 1 Maccabees. "Finally, Judah fell and the surviving Jews fled."

With Judah dead, Bacchides felt secure enough to allow Simon and Jonathan, under a truce, to take their dead brother's body and bury it in Modin. Bacchides was so certain that the Judean revolt had ended with the death of Judah that he allowed a protracted public mourning. "And they bewailed him," writes the author of 1 Maccabees, "and all Israel made great lamentation for him and mourned many days, and said: 'How is our champion fallen, the savior of Israel!' "

But the struggle for Judean independence went on, led by Judah's three surviving brothers, John, Jonathan, and Simon. Jonathan was chosen to lead the resistance to the Seleucids. John was killed

Above left, the death of Judah Maccabee at the Battle of Elasa in 160 B.C., as depicted in a 12th-century Bible. Above right, the three surviving Maccabee brothers prepare Judah's body for burial. Bacchides, the victorious Seleucid general, allowed a period of national mourning for Judah throughout Judea.

shortly thereafter while trying to contact the Nabataeans, the Judeans' allies. The high priest Almus died in 159 B.C., and the Seleucids were unable to install a replacement for seven years. In 157 B.C., Jonathan's army defeated Bacchides, prompting the latter to slaughter hundreds of Jewish Hellenizers, whom he blamed for the 10 years of open warfare in Judea. He signed a peace treaty with Jonathan, who ruled the province and suppressed the Hellenizing party for the next five years. In 152 B.C. a struggle for the Seleucid throne between Demetrius I and a challenger, Alexander Balas, was exploited by Jonathan, who supported Demetrius I in exchange for the right to occupy Jerusalem. Two years later, Alexander Balas made a higher bid for Jonathan's support and appointed him high priest; when Alexander Balas overthrew Demetrius I and killed him, he made Jonathan governor of the province and a general of the Seleucid army. Jonathan expanded Judean territory beyond the province's previous borders and began to incorporate the neighboring states in Palestine.

In 143 B.C. Jonathan was killed by an aspirant to the Seleucid throne, and Simon, the last of the Maccabee brothers, assumed the leadership of Judea. He took advantage of yet another Seleucid power struggle, between Demetrius II and Diodotus Tryphon, by agreeing to support Demetrius II in exchange for the granting of complete political independence for Judea. In 142 B.C. Judea became an independent nation with Simon ruling as high priest, commander, and leader. He expelled all the remaining Seleucid garrisons — including the one in the Acra, which had withstood so many Jewish sieges and assaults for more than a quarter century. Judea was now totally free. Simon ruled for another eight years, the first of the Hashmonean leaders of Judea.

The Maccabees' struggle against Hellenism had lasted for 25 years, but ironically, Hashmonean rulers governed in the style of Hellenistic monarchs, engaging in power struggles, amassing great wealth, and assembling armies whose mission was to keep the ruler on the throne as much as it was

In 157 B.C., Jonathan, who succeeded Judah as military, political, and religious leader of Judea, defeated Bacchides, ending Seleucid efforts to crush the Jews. In 142 B.C., Simon, the last surviving Maccabee brother, gained complete independence for Judea and founded the Hashmonean line of kings.

to further the interests of the state. Judea, having conquered most of its neighboring territory and having converted many of its neighboring peoples to Judaism, now included almost all of Palestine. The Samaritan temple was destroyed, the Idumaeans became Jews and emerged as an important factor in Judean politics, and around 100 B.C. a Hashmonean first took the title of king. The successors to the Hasidic party, which by this time had fragmented into a number of parties dedicated to a strict interpretation of orthodox Judaism, objected to the Hellenized rule of the Hashmoneans.

Meanwhile, the Roman Empire continued to expand, conquering the crumbling Seleucid Empire in 65 B.C. Two years later the Romans marched into Judea and took Jerusalem, massacring thousands of its inhabitants. Judea was once again reduced to the status of a small province under the rule of a mighty empire, though it still enjoyed some freedom in religious and local matters. Fired by the memory of the Maccabees' successful struggle against the Seleucids, zealous Jews rebelled time and again against the Romans. Finally, after a failed

A Hashmonean coin minted around 40 B.C. For almost 2,000 years, the Jewish people have remembered Judah's religious piety and military ability. In 1948, with the establishment of the modern nation of Israel, the ideal of an independent Jewish state was realized for the first time since the days of the Maccabees.

revolt in 70 A.D., the Romans sacked the Temple, destroyed it, wrecked the city, removed all vestiges of political autonomy, and deported most of Judea's population from the province. Another revolt in the year 135 was crushed and the Romans responded by banning all Jews from entering Jerusalem. The remaining Jews in Palestine were deported and dispersed far away in lands throughout the empire. Hundreds of years would elapse before any would return, and more than 1,800 years would pass before the Jews ruled in their holy land again.

Through all these events, the name of Judah Maccabee lived on, reverberating through history. In addition to providing an example to the zealots who defied Rome, the mystical faith in the righteousness of the Maccabean cause helped fuel the belief in the imminent arrival of a messiah. Portions of the Book of Daniel, which forms part of the Old Testament, were written around 165 B.C., during the worst days of Antiochus IV's anti-Jewish measures, and reflect a sense of impending horror, violent struggle, and the need to trust in God. It presents the concept of a messiah in terms never before seen in Jewish literature; 2 Maccabees, with its visions of angelic armies fighting alongside the righteous, also reflects a new, more mystical element in Jewish writings. A century and a half after the Maccabean struggle, there were several sects of Jews living in seclusion or otherwise trying to attain purity in expectation of another clash between the forces of good and evil. This element in Jewish thought, so profoundly affected by the Maccabean struggle, found its way into Christianity and formed a basis for that offshoot of the Jewish religion.

The Books of the Maccabees thus became accepted as part of the New Testament of the Christian Bible. But they never became an accepted part of Jews' holy writings. The rabbis who lived after the dispersion of the Jews from Palestine regarded the Hashmonean kings as an unholy line of rulers whose ultimate acceptance of worldly politics and Hellenistic customs violated the Law. The rabbis held that the Hashmonean kings were largely responsible for the expulsion of the Jews from their holy land. Eventually, the celebration of Nicanor's

Day, one of the two holidays introduced by Judah, was abandoned.

The other, Hanukkah, continued throughout the centuries, but the character of its observance changed. The emphasis was no longer placed on the military, nationalistic aspects of the holiday. Instead the Talmudic tale of the miraculous burning of one day's worth of oil for eight days took prominence, and the holiday slowly became an innocuous, gift-giving celebration. It was only with the rise of Zionism, the 19th and 20th century movement advocating the return of Jews to Palestine, that the more nationalistic side of the holiday was revived. With the establishment of the modern state of Israel in 1948, the military exploits of Judah Maccabee once again were placed in the forefront during the celebration of Hanukkah. And in the late 1970s, the Israeli government would point to the boundaries of Simon's Judea, which encompassed most of Palestine, to justify in part the establishment of Jewish settlements in the West Bank.

Today, more than 21 centuries after Judah Maccabee led the revolt against the Seleucid Empire, one of the ways Jewish children celebrate Hanukkah is by playing with a small, four-sided top called a *dreidel*. On the four sides of the dreidel are imprinted the Hebrew letters *nun*, *gimel*, *hay*, and *shin* (*N*, *G*, *H*, and *Sh*), which stand for a Hebrew phrase that recalls the Maccabean triumph in the face of overwhelming odds:

"A great miracle happened there."

# Further Reading

*The Apocrypha.* Oxford: Oxford University Press, 1963.

Bar-Kochva, Bezalel. *The Seleucid Army.* Cambridge: Cambridge University Press, 1976.

Bickerman, Elias. *From Ezra to the Last of the Maccabees.* New York: Schocken Books, 1962.

————. *The Maccabees: An Account of Their History from the Beginnings to the Fall of the House of the Hasmoneans.* New York: Schocken Books, 1947.

Conder, Claude Reignier. *Judas Maccabaeus and the Jewish War of Independence.* London: A. P. Watt & Son, 1893.

Farmer, William Reuben. *Maccabees, Zealots, and Josephus.* New York: Columbia University Press, 1956.

Gardner, Joseph L. *Atlas of the Bible.* Pleasantville, NY: Reader's Digest Press, 1981.

Goldstein, Jonathan A. *The Anchor Bible Translation and Commentary* on *I & II Maccabees.* Garden City, NY: Doubleday, 1983.

Hengle, Martin. *Jews, Greeks and Barbarians.* Philadelphia: Fortress Press, 1980.

Josephus, Flavius. *Jewish Antiquities.* Books 12 and 13. Cambridge, MA: Harvard University Press, 1942.

Michener, James A. *The Source.* New York: Fawcett Books, 1978.

Patten, Priscilla, and Rebecca Patten. *Before the Times.* San Francisco: Strawberry Hill Press, 1980.

Pearlman, Moshe. *The Maccabees.* Jerusalem: Weidenfeld and Nicolson, 1973.

Russell, D. S. *The Jews from Alexander to Herod.* Oxford: Oxford University Press, 1967.

Schalit, Abraham. *The World History of the Jewish People.* Vol. 6, *The Hellenistic Age.* Jerusalem: Weidenfeld and Nicolson, 1973.

Simon, Norma. *Hanukkah.* New York: Harper & Row, 1966.

Wright, Ernest G. *Great People of the Bible and How They Lived.* Pleasantville, NY: Reader's Digest Press, 1974.

Zeitlin, Solomon. *The Rise and Fall of the Judean State.* Philadelphia: Jewish Publication Society of America, 1968.

# Chronology

# Index

**E. H. Fortier** received his bachelor of science degree in Biblical theology from Patten Bible College, where he taught for four years. He also holds a bachelor's degree in history from Azusa Pacific University and a master's degree from Holy Names College. He lives in Oakland, California.

**Arthur M. Schlesinger, jr.,** taught history at Harvard for many years and is currently Albert Schweitzer Professor of the Humanities at City University of New York. He is the author of numerous highly praised works in American history and has twice been awarded the Pulitzer Prize. He served in the White House as special assistant to Presidents Kennedy and Johnson.

PICTURE CREDITS